elevate science

SAVVAS
LEARNING COMPANY

You are an author!

This is your book to keep. Write and draw in it! Record your data and discoveries in it! You are an author of this book!

Print your name, school, town, and state below.

My Photo

Name

School

Town, State

LEARNING COMPANY

ISBN-13:   978-0-328-94873-4
ISBN-10:   0-328-94873-X

6 - 20

Program Authors

ZIPPORAH MILLER, EdD

Coordinator for K-12 Science Programs, Anne Arundel County Public Schools.
Zipporah Miller currently serves as the Senior Manager for Organizational Learning with the Anne Arundel County Public School System. Prior to that she served as the K-12 Coordinator for science in Anne Arundel County. She conducts national training to science stakeholders on the Next Generation Science Standards. Dr. Miller also served as the Associate Executive Director for Professional Development Programs and conferences at the National Science Teachers Association (NSTA) and served as a reviewer during the development of Next Generation Science Standards. Dr. Miller holds a doctoral degree from University of Maryland College Park, a master's degree in school administration and supervision from Bowie State University, and a bachelor's degree from Chadron State College.

MICHAEL J. PADILLA, PhD

Professor Emeritus, Eugene P. Moore School of Education, Clemson University, Clemson, South Carolina
Michael J. Padilla taught science in middle and secondary schools, has more than 30 years of experience educating middle grades science teachers, and served as one of the writers of the 1996 U.S. National Science Education Standards. In recent years Mike has focused on teaching science to English Language Learners. His extensive leadership experience, serving as Principal Investigator on numerous National Science Foundation and U.S. Department of Education grants, resulted in more than $35 million in funding to improve science education. He served as president of the National Science Teachers Association, the world's largest science teaching organization, in 2005–6.

MICHAEL E. WYSESSION, PhD

Professor of Earth and Planetary Sciences, Washington University, St. Louis, Missouri
An author on more than 100 science and science education publications, Dr. Wysession was awarded the prestigious National Science Foundation Presidential Faculty Fellowship and Packard Foundation Fellowship for his research in geophysics, primarily focused on using seismic tomography to determine the forces driving plate tectonics. Dr. Wysession is also a leader in geoscience literacy and education, including being chair of the Earth Science Literacy Principles, author of several popular geology Great Courses video lecture series, and a lead writer of the Next Generation Science Standards*.

Reviewers

Program Consultants

Carol Baker
Science Curriculum

Dr. Carol K. Baker is superintendent for Lyons Elementary K-8 School District in Lyons, Illinois. Prior to that, she was Director of Curriculum for Science and Music in Oak Lawn, Illinois. Before that she taught Physics and Earth Science for 18 years. In the recent past, Dr. Baker also wrote assessment questions for ACT (EXPLORE and PLAN), was elected president of the Illinois Science Teachers Association from 2011-2013 and served as a member of the Museum of Science and Industry advisory boards in Chicago. She is a writer of the Next Generation Science Standards. Dr. Baker received her BS in Physics and a science teaching certification. She completed her Master of Educational Administration (K-12) and earned her doctorate in Educational Leadership.

Jim Cummins
ELL

Dr. Cummins's research focuses on literacy development in multilingual schools and the role technology plays in learning across the curriculum. *Elevate Science* incorporates research-based principles for integrating language with the teaching of academic content based on Dr. Cummins's work.

Elfrieda Hiebert
Literacy

Dr. Hiebert is the President and CEO of TextProject, a nonprofit aimed at providing open-access resources for instruction of beginning and struggling readers, and a former primary school teacher. She is also a research associate at the University of California Santa Cruz. Her research addresses how fluency, vocabulary, and knowledge can be fostered through appropriate texts, and her contributions have been recognized through awards, such as the Oscar Causey Award for Outstanding Contributions to Reading Research (Literacy Research Association, 2015), Research to Practice Award (American Educational Research Association, 2013), William S. Gray Citation of Merit Award for Outstanding Contributions to Reading Research (International Reading Association, 2008).

Content Reviewers

Alex Blom, Ph.D.
Associate Professor
Department Of Physical Sciences
Alverno College
Milwaukee, Wisconsin

Joy Branlund, Ph.D.
Department of Physical Science
Southwestern Illinois College
Granite City, Illinois

Judy Calhoun
Associate Professor
Physical Sciences
Alverno College
Milwaukee, Wisconsin

Stefan Debbert
Associate Professor of Chemistry
Lawrence University
Appleton, Wisconsin

Diane Doser
Professor
Department of Geological Sciences
University of Texas at El Paso
El Paso, Texas

Rick Duhrkopf, Ph. D.
Department of Biology
Baylor University
Waco, Texas

Jennifer Liang
University Of Minnesota Duluth
Duluth, Minnesota

Heather Mernitz, Ph.D.
Associate Professor of Physical
Sciences
Alverno College
Milwaukee, Wisconsin

Joseph McCullough, Ph.D.
Cabrillo College
Aptos, California

Katie M. Nemeth, Ph.D.
Assistant Professor
College of Science and Engineering
University of Minnesota Duluth
Duluth, Minnesota

Maik Pertermann
Department of Geology
Western Wyoming Community College
Rock Springs, Wyoming

Scott Rochette
Department of the Earth Sciences
The College at Brockport
State University of New York
Brockport, New York

David Schuster
Washington University in St Louis
St. Louis, Missouri

Shannon Stevenson
Department of Biology
University of Minnesota Duluth
Duluth, Minnesota

Paul Stoddard, Ph.D.
Department of Geology and
Environmental Geosciences
Northern Illinois University
DeKalb, Illinois

Nancy Taylor
American Public University
Charles Town, West Virginia

Safety Reviewers

Douglas Mandt, M.S.
Science Education Consultant
Edgewood, Washington

Juliana Textley, Ph.D.
Author, NSTA books on school
science safety
Adjunct Professor
Lesley University
Cambridge, Massachusetts

Teacher Reviewers

Jennifer Bennett, M.A.
Memorial Middle School
Tampa, Florida

Sonia Blackstone
Lake County Schools
Howey In the Hills, Florida

Teresa Bode
Roosevelt Elementary
Tampa, Florida

Tyler C. Britt, Ed.S.
Curriculum & Instructional
 Practice Coordinator
Raytown Quality Schools
Raytown, Missouri

A. Colleen Campos
Grandview High School
Aurora, Colorado

Coleen Doulk
Challenger School
Spring Hill, Florida

Mary D. Dube
Burnett Middle School
Seffner, Florida

Sandra Galpin
Adams Middle School
Tampa, Florida

Margaret Henry
Lebanon Junior High School
Lebanon, Ohio

Christina Hill
Beth Shields Middle School
Ruskin, Florida

Judy Johnis
Gorden Burnett Middle School
Seffner, Florida

Karen Y. Johnson
Beth Shields Middle School
Ruskin, Florida

Jane Kemp
Lockhart Elementary School
Tampa, Florida

Denise Kuhling
Adams Middle School
Tampa, Florida

Esther Leonard M.Ed. and L.M.T.
Gifted and Talented Implementation Specialist
San Antonio Independent School District
San Antonio, Texas

Kelly Maharaj
Science Department Chairperson
Challenger K8 School of Science and
 Mathematics
Elgin, Florida

Kevin J. Maser, Ed.D.
H. Frank Carey Jr/Sr High School
Franklin Square, New York

Angie L. Matamoros, Ph.D.
ALM Science Consultant
Weston, Florida

Corey Mayle
Brogden Middle School
Durham, North Carolina

Keith McCarthy
George Washington Middle School
Wayne, New Jersey

Yolanda O. Peña
John F. Kennedy Junior High School
West Valley City, Utah

Kathleen M. Poe
Jacksonville Beach Elementary School
Jacksonville Beach, Florida

Wendy Rauld
Monroe Middle School
Tampa, Florida

Bryna Selig
Gaithersburg Middle School
Gaithersburg, Maryland

Pat (Patricia) Shane, Ph.D.
STEM & ELA Education Consultant
Chapel Hill, North Carolina

Diana Shelton
Burnett Middle School
Seffner, Florida

Nakia Sturrup
Jennings Middle School
Seffner, Florida

Melissa Triebwasser
Walden Lake Elementary
Plant City, Florida

Michele Bubley Wiehagen
Science Coach
Miles Elementary School
Tampa, Florida

Pauline Wilcox
Instructional Science Coach
Fox Chapel Middle School
Spring Hill, Florida

Sound

1-PS4-1, 1-PS4-4,
K-2-ETS1-1

Quest

In this Quest activity, you meet an orchestra conductor. She needs your help. She needs to send a secret message to a friend in the back of a music hall. She will use a sound code to send the message.

Like an orchestra conductor, you will complete activities and labs. You will use what you learn in the lessons to make a secret sound code. Then you will send a message using the code.

Find your Quest activities on pages 10, 18, and 25.

Career Connection Orchestra Conductor on page 29

VIDEO

eTEXT

INTERACTIVITY

SCIENCE SONG

GAME

DOCUMENT

ASSESSMENT

HANDS-ON LAB

Topic 2

Light

1-PS4-2, 1-PS4-3, 1-PS4-4, K-2-ETS1-1

Quest

In this Quest activity, you meet a game designer. He needs your help. He wants to send secret messages using light. Players will use the light messages in a laser tag game.

Like a game designer, you will complete activities and labs. You will use what you learn in the lessons to write a guide for using secret light messages. People can use the guide in a laser tag game.

Find your Quest activities on pages 47, 54, and 64.

Career Connection Storm Chaser on page 67

- ▶ **VIDEO**
- 📖 **eTEXT**
- 👆 **INTERACTIVITY**
- 🎮 **GAME**
- 📄 **DOCUMENT**
- ☑ **ASSESSMENT**

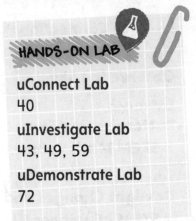

HANDS-ON LAB

Topic 3

Sky and Earth

1-ESS1-1, 1-ESS1-2, K-2-ETS1-1, K-2-ETS1-2

Quest

In this Quest activity, you meet a space scientist. She needs your help. She wants you to find a way to tell students about patterns in the sky.

Like the space scientist, you will complete activities and labs. You will use what you learn in the lessons to write a play about sky patterns.

Find your Quest activities on pages 85, 92, and 98.

Career Connection Space Scientist on page 103

VIDEO

eTEXT

INTERACTIVITY

SCIENCE SONG

GAME

DOCUMENT

ASSESSMENT

The Essential Question

HANDS-ON LAB

1-ESS1-2

Weather and Seasons

Quest

In this Quest activity, you meet a meteorologist. He needs your help. He wants to make a trip guide. It will use information about weather to show families the best place and time of year to take trips.

Like the meteorologist, you will complete activities and labs. You will use what you learn in the lessons to design a trip guide. Then you can make it.

Find your Quest activities on pages 122 and 132.

Career Connection Meteorologist on page 135

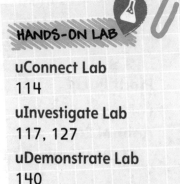

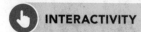 VIDEO

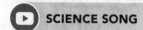 eTEXT

INTERACTIVITY

 SCIENCE SONG

 GAME

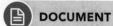 DOCUMENT

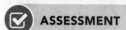 ASSESSMENT

HANDS-ON LAB

Living Things

1-LS1-1, K-2-ETS1-1, K-2-ETS1, K-2-ETS1-3

Quest

In this **STEM** Quest activity, you meet a bioengineer. She wants you to think of a problem people have. Then you will find a way to use a plant or animal part to help solve the problem.

Like the bioengineer, you will complete activities and labs. Use what you learn in the lessons to find a plant or animal part that will help solve a human problem.

Find your Quest activities on pages 153, 159, 166, and 174.

Career Connection Bioengineer on page 177

VIDEO

eTEXT

INTERACTIVITY

SCIENCE SONG

GAME

DOCUMENT

ASSESSMENT

HANDS-ON LAB

Parents and Offspring

1-LS1-2, 1-LS3-1

 VIDEO

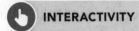 eTEXT

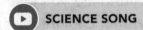 INTERACTIVITY

 SCIENCE SONG

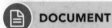 GAME

DOCUMENT

ASSESSMENT

Quest

In this Quest activity, you meet a nature scientist. She has a problem. Some animals have escaped from the zoo. Help her find the parents of three young animals.

Like the nature scientist, you will complete activities and labs. You will use what you learn in the lessons to match the adult animals with their young. Then you will make a model of an adult and young animal.

Find your Quest activities on pages 194, 203, and 214.

Career Connection nature scientist on page 217

HANDS-ON LAB

Elevate your thinking!

Elevate Science takes science to a whole new level and lets you take ownership of your learning. Explore science in the world around you. Investigate how things work. Think critically and solve problems! *Elevate Science* helps you think like a scientist, so you're ready for a world of discoveries.

Explore Your World

Explore real-life scenarios with engaging Quests that dig into science topics around the world. You can:

- Solve real-world problems
- Apply skills and knowledge
- Communicate solutions

Quest Kickoff

Find the Parents

What clues help us find a young animal's parent?

Make Connections

Elevate Science connects science to other subjects and shows you how to better understand the world through:

- Mathematics
- Reading and Writing
- Literacy

Literacy ▸ Toolbox

Main Ideas and Details All living things grow and change is the main idea. Use the details to tell how a watermelon plant changes during its life cycle.

Math ▸ Toolbox

Compare Numbers You can compare how long objects are. Parent rabbits have longer ears than young rabbits. Use cubes to measure the lengths of two classroom objects. Which is longer?

Connecting Concepts ▸ Toolbox

Patterns Nature has many patterns. A **pattern** is something that repeats. Parents protect their young. They use their bodies to protect them. What patterns do you see on these two pages?

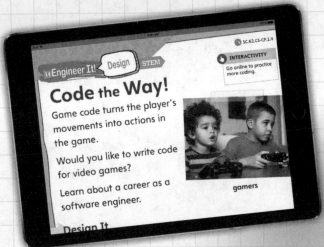

Build Skills for the Future

- Master the Engineering Design Process
- Apply critical thinking and analytical skills
- Learn about STEM careers

Focus on Reading Skills

Elevate Science creates ongoing reading connections to help you develop the reading skills you need to succeed. Features include:

- Leveled Readers
- Literacy Connection Features
- Reading Checks

Literacy Connection

Main Idea and Details

Nature scientists observe animals. Read about the main idea and details of geese and their young.

The main idea is what the sentences are about. Details tell about the main idea.

GAME
Practice what you learn with the Toolbox Games.

Enter the Lab

Hands-on experiments and virtual labs help you test ideas and show what you know in performance-based assessments. Scaffolded labs include:

- STEM Labs
- Design Your Own
- Open-ended Labs

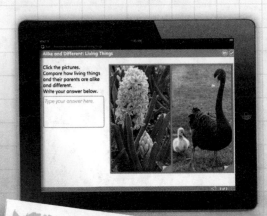

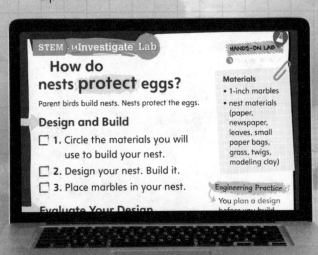

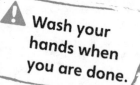

Sound

Next Generation Science Standards

1-PS4-1. Plan and conduct investigations to provide evidence that vibrating materials can make sound and that sound can make materials vibrate.

1-PS4-4. Use tools and materials to design and build a device that uses light or sound to solve the problem of communicating over a distance.

K-2-ETS1-1: Ask questions, make observations, and gather information about a situation people want to change to define a simple problem that can be solved through the development of a new or improved object or tool.

The Essential Question

What happens when objects vibrate?

Show What You Know

Which instruments make loud sounds when you bang on them? Circle them.

Quest Kickoff

Sending Sound Messages

How can you use sound to send a secret code?

Phenomenon Shhh! This is a secret. My name is Miss Keene. I am a conductor of an orchestra. I need to send a message to a friend. She is in the back of the music hall. The message is secret. It has to be sent through sound.

Can you help me? I need help thinking of a code as a way to send my message. Look for clues as you read. The path shows the Quest activities you will complete as you work through the topic. Check off your progress each time you complete an activity with a **QUEST CHECK ✓ OFF** .

Next Generation Science Standards

1-PS4-4. Use tools and materials to design and build a device that uses light or sound to solve the problem of communicating over a distance. **K-2-ETS1-1:** Ask questions, make observations, and gather information about a situation people want to change to define a simple problem that can be solved through the development of a new or improved object or tool.

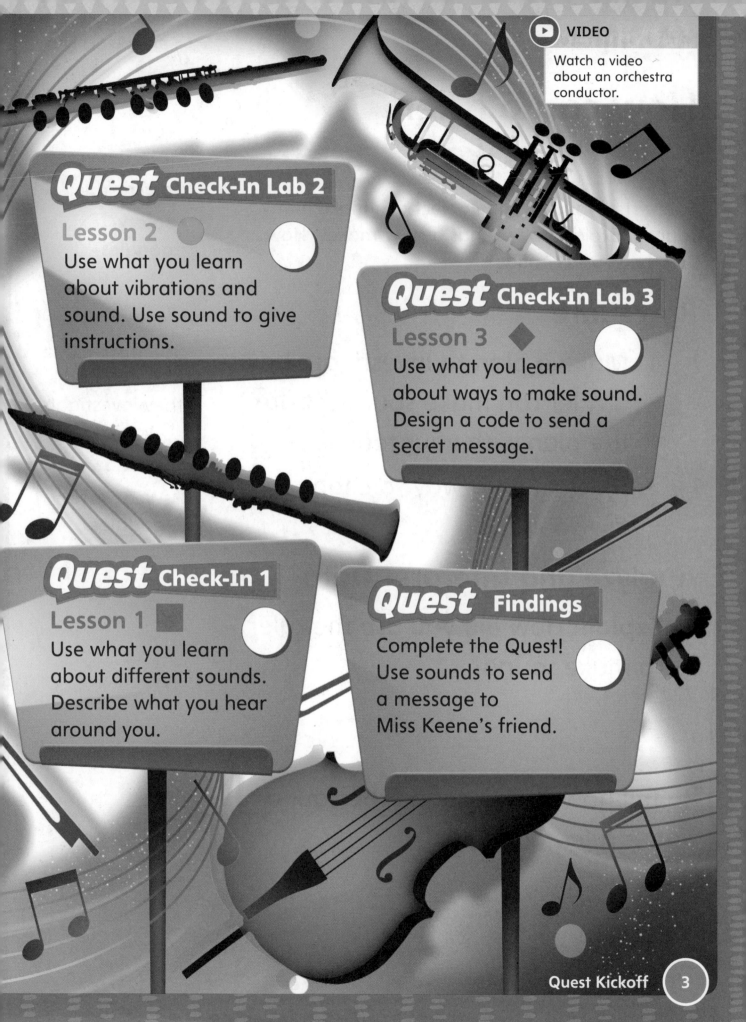

▶ VIDEO

Watch a video about an orchestra conductor.

Quest Check-In Lab 2

Lesson 2

Use what you learn about vibrations and sound. Use sound to give instructions.

Quest Check-In Lab 3

Lesson 3 ◆

Use what you learn about ways to make sound. Design a code to send a secret message.

Quest Check-In 1

Lesson 1 ■

Use what you learn about different sounds. Describe what you hear around you.

Quest Findings

Complete the Quest! Use sounds to send a message to Miss Keene's friend.

HANDS-ON LAB

1-PS4-1, SEP.3, CCC.2

How can a ruler make a sound?

Scientists know that one object can make many sounds. Explore the sounds a ruler makes. How can the sound change?

Materials
- plastic ruler
- safety goggles

Procedure

☐ 1. **Make a plan** to investigate how a ruler can make sound. Share the plan with your teacher.

☐ 2. Investigate a way to change the sound.

Science Practice

Scientists make a plan before they investigate.

⚠ **Wear safety goggles.**

Analyze and Interpret Data

3. **Explain** How did you use the ruler to make sound?

_____

_ _ _ _ _ _ _ _ _ _ _ _ _ _ _ _ _ _ _

_____

4. **Tell** how you changed the sound the ruler made.

Draw Conclusions

Scientists draw conclusions from details. Read about a marching band in a parade. Then draw your own conclusion.

🎮 GAME

Practice what you learn with the Mini Games.

Jesse heard music. It was very soft. The musicians came around the corner. They marched in front of where Jesse stood on the sidewalk. Now the music was very loud! The band marched on. Jesse watched the band march far away.

☑ **Reading Check** **Draw Conclusions**

How did the band sound when it marched far away?

_____

_____

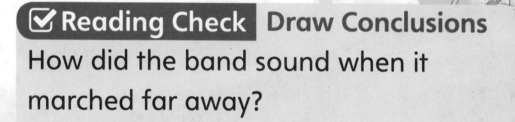

Describe Sound

Vocabulary

vibrate
pitch
volume

I can describe sound.

1-PS4-1, K-2-ETS1-1

Jumpstart Discovery!

Use your voice to make different sounds. Take turns describing the sounds with a partner.

How does size affect sound?

Musicians make different sounds by changing the length of an instrument. How can you use length to change sound?

Materials

- 8 straws
- tape
- scissors
- ruler

Procedure

☐ 1. **Make a model** to test how length changes sound by using all of the materials.

☐ 2. Test your model.

☐ 3. **Observe** the sounds and the vibrations.

☐ 4. Play a tune using your model.

Science Practice

Scientists **use models** to understand how things work.

 Be careful using scissors.

Analyze and Interpret Data

5. **Compare** How are the sounds of the straws different?

shorter is higher pitched and longer is lower pitched

6. Talk to a partner. Tell how your breath is making sound.

Sound

Sound is energy you can hear. Bang a drum. What do you hear? You hear sound. What do you feel? The top of the drum vibrates. Sound comes from objects that vibrate. **Vibrate** means to move back and forth very quickly.

☑ Reading Check **Draw Conclusions**
You pluck a violin string. Tell what happens.

Pitch and Volume

INTERACTIVITY

Compare the pitch and volume of sounds.

The way objects sound can be high or low. Sounds can be different pitches. **Pitch** is how high or low a sound is.

The way objects sound can be loud or soft. **Volume** is how loud or soft a sound is.

Draw something that makes a loud sound. Draw something that makes a soft sound.

Loud Sound	Soft Sound

Quest Connection

How could you use pitch and volume in a secret message?

Sounds of the World

Animals use sound to send messages, too. Sound helps them stay alive.

A coyote howls to warn other animals to stay away. A howl has a high pitch.

A mother coyote growls to get her pups' attention. A growl has a low pitch.

A pack of coyotes may bark. Their bark is loud.

Draw Conclusions

Think of an animal in nature. What sounds does it make?
Why do you think it makes those sounds?

_____

_____

_____

_____

_____

Echolocation

Bats use sound in another way. They make a sound only they can hear. The sound bounces off objects. Bats hear where the objects are. Bats do not see well. They use sound to help them see at night.

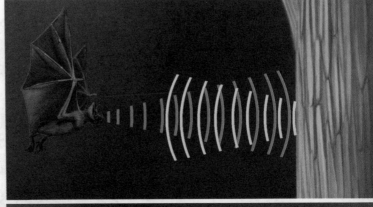

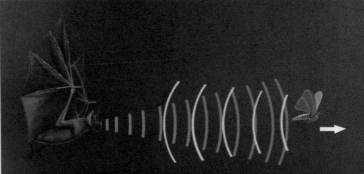

Have you ever made an echo? Then you bounced your voice off an object, too.

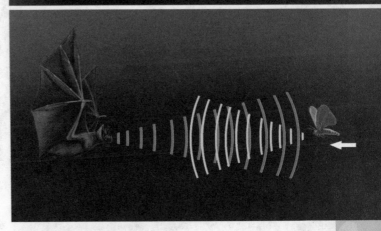

Listen Close your eyes. Have a partner silently move away from you. Clap your hands. When your partner claps back, move toward the sound. Can you catch your partner?

Make Sound

▶ **VIDEO**

Watch a video about how vibrations make sound.

Vocabulary

percussion

I can vibrate objects to make sounds.

I can show that sounds can make objects vibrate.

1-PS4-1

Jumpstart Discovery!

Put your lips together.
Blow air. What do you hear?
What do you feel?

How can you see sound?

Sound is something that you hear. Scientists find ways to see sound to study it better. How can you see sound?

Procedure

☐ 1. Use the cup, string, and plastic wrap to make a drum.

☐ 2. Sprinkle sand on the plastic wrap. Move close to the surface of the cup. Hum loudly. Hum softly. Record your observations.

Materials

• plastic cup
• string
• clear plastic wrap
• sand
• safety goggles

 Wear safety goggles.

Science Practice

Scientists use **evidence** to support an idea or argument.

Observations

Analyze and Interpret Data

3. **Explain** Tell what evidence let you see sound.

Making Sounds

👆 **INTERACTIVITY**

Compare how long and short strings make different sounds.

Every sound makes a vibration. Put your hands on your throat. Sing! Vocal cords vibrate in the throat. They help us sing or speak.

Put your hands on your throat again. Describe what you feel when your voice changes pitch.

The short bars on a xylophone make a high pitch. The long bars on a xylophone make a low pitch.

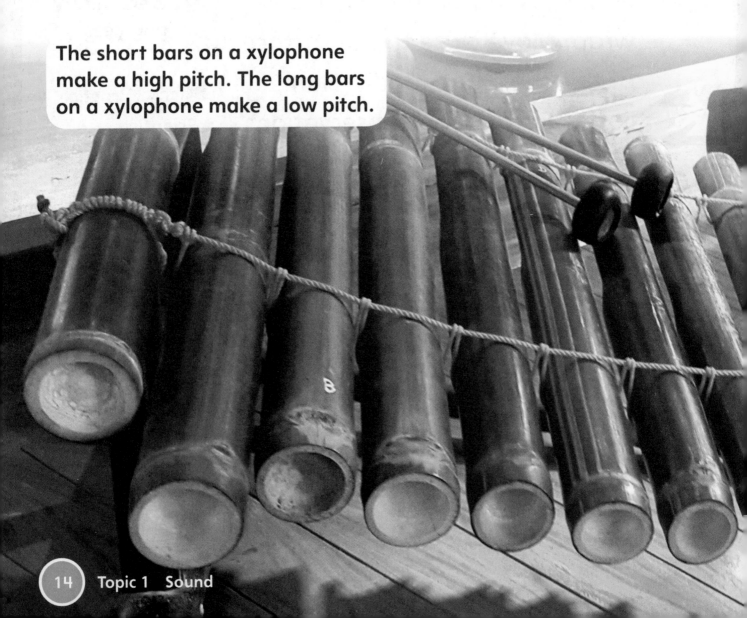

Musical Sounds

Similar instruments can make different sounds.

Large instruments with long strings can make lower sounds. Small instruments with shorter strings can make higher sounds.

A violin is small. It has short strings.

A cello is large. It has long strings.

Making Music

Some instruments have strings. You pull the strings. The strings vibrate.

You blow into some instruments. The air inside of them vibrates in a special way. These are called wind instruments.

You strike some instruments to make them vibrate. Drums, bells, and tambourines are instruments you strike to make sound. Drums, cymbals, and xylophones are called percussion instruments. **Percussion** instruments are ones you strike to make sound.

Visual Literacy Choose an instrument. Which part of it vibrates to make sound? Circle that part.

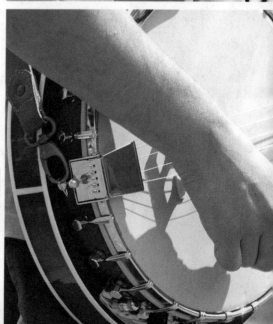

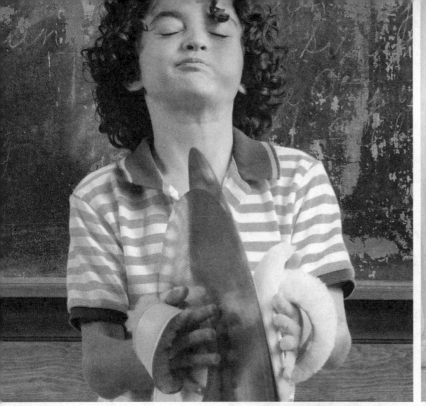

Quest Connection

Music from some instruments can be heard from far away. How can this help you send a message?

How can instruments talk?

Objects that vibrate make different sounds. Conductors listen as the instruments are played to make music. How can you listen and use sounds to tell your classmates how to move?

Suggested Materials

- rubber spatula
- wooden spoon
- whisk
- metal box
- plastic container
- metal baking tray

Procedure

☐ **1.** Make a plan to test the sound of different objects. Share the plan with your teacher.

☐ **2.** Test ways to make the objects vibrate.

☐ **3.** Assign a movement to do when you make each sound. This is your secret code.

☐ **4.** Write down your secret code in the chart.

☐ **5.** Try your code with a partner.

Science Practice

Scientists **investigate** something to see how it works.

Observations

Objects Used	Describe the sound made.	Movement for the sound

Analyze and Interpret Data

6. **Compare** your results with another group. Tell why some objects would make good instruments to send a secret message.

Lesson 3

Uses of Sound

▶ **VIDEO**

Watch a video about the different ways sound is used to communicate.

Vocabulary

communicate

I can identify how people use sounds.

1-PS4-4

Jumpstart Discovery!

Say something in a normal voice to a partner. Roll a piece of paper into a tube or cone. Say the same thing the same way into the tube. What does the paper do to the sound?

What does that sound say? ● ● ◼ ●

Morse code uses sounds to make words. Dots are short sounds. Dashes are long sounds. How can you use Morse code to make words?

Procedure

☐ 1. Plan what you want to say using Morse code.

☐ 2. Choose the best materials to make long and short sounds.

☐ 3. Tap your message.

Analyze and Interpret Data

4. **Explain** which objects worked best to make long and short sounds?

5. **Explain** what it was like to make a message using Morse code. What was it like to understand a message?

Suggested Materials

- keyboard
- digital chimes
- drumsticks
- Morse code

Science Practice

Scientists construct an explanation after they investigate.

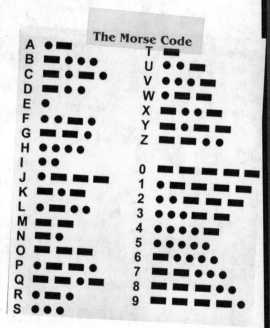

The Morse Code

Using Sounds

INTERACTIVITY

Compare how peoples of the past used sound to communicate over long distances.

We use sound to communicate. **Communicate** means to share information.

People first used drums and bells to send messages. The sound traveled long distances. It also took a long time. Messages had to be simple.

Tell How have you used sound to communicate today?

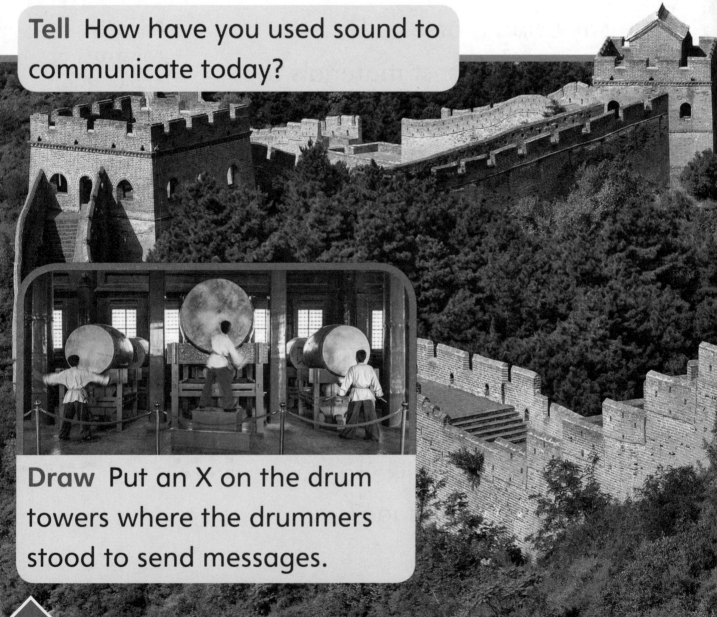

Draw Put an X on the drum towers where the drummers stood to send messages.

Phones were invented later. The first phones could make calls close by. The sound was not very good.

Draw a circle around phones that you have used.

The Great Wall of China

Communicating with Sound

Today, it is easy to connect far away. We still use phones. We also use satellites and computers. Today, many families and friends live far apart. Computers and phones are important ways families and friends can stay connected.

Literacy ▸ Toolbox

Draw Conclusions
How do you communicate with friends and family that live far away? Why is it important to be able to communicate sound over long distances?

Quest Connection

How can you send a message using music?

How can an instrument *send a secret?*

You have used objects to make different sounds. You have used sounds to send messages. How can you make a device or an instrument to send a secret message?

Suggested Materials

- plastic cup
- plastic wrap
- sand
- rubber spatula
- wooden spoon
- whisk
- metal box
- plastic container
- metal baking tray
- glue or tape
- craft sticks
- paper clips

Design

☐ 1. Choose a few objects to work with.

☐ 2. Plan out a device or instrument, think of a message, and make a code.

☐ 3. Practice using the code and the objects.

Engineering Practice

Engineers design solutions to problems in the real world.

Evaluate Your Design

4. **Explain** How will your message sound from far away?

_____

_____

K-2-ETS1-1, SEP.6

INTERACTIVITY

Go online to learn about other types of alerts.

Alert! Alert!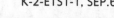

Phenomenon Smart phones use sound. There is a sound for everything! Each sound means something different. Phones ring when someone calls. A ding can be for a new message. Alarms may beep.

Improve It

You hear three loud beeps from your phone. This tells you that bad weather is nearby and to take shelter. What if your phone was not nearby?

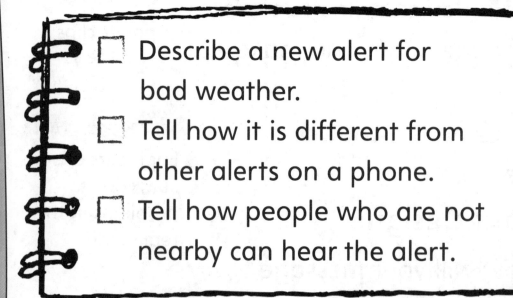

☐ Describe a new alert for bad weather.

☐ Tell how it is different from other alerts on a phone.

☐ Tell how people who are not nearby can hear the alert.

1. What kind of weather is the alert for?

2. What will the alert sound like?

3. Will there be follow-up alerts?

STEM Sending Sound Messages

How can you use sound to send a secret code?

Phenomenon Think about what you learned in this topic. Use a secret sound code you made or make up a new one. Send your secret sound code to a partner that is far away. Send your message to your partner.

Show What You Found

Compare your secret sound code with a different partner. Tell how the secret sound codes are similar. Explain how they are different.

QUEST CHECK ✓ OFF

Orchestra Conductor

Conductors know a lot about the science of sound. They know how vibrations make sound. They know how to make instruments have high and low pitches.

Conductors also work with sound engineers. Sound engineers make sure that everyone can hear the beautiful music the conductor and the musicians are making.

Why is it important to have a leader of an orchestra?

_____

_____

_____

_____

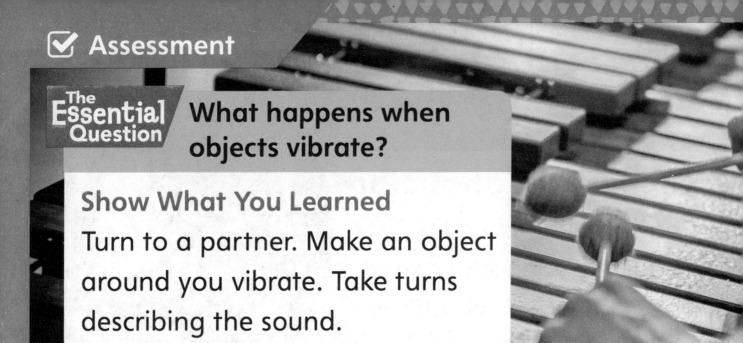

The Essential Question What happens when objects vibrate?

Show What You Learned

Turn to a partner. Make an object around you vibrate. Take turns describing the sound.

1. Decide if each statement about sound is true or false. Circle the one that is false.

   a. Sound is energy you can hear.

   b. Sound makes vibrations.

   c. When objects vibrate, they make sound.

   d. Only music can communicate with sound.

2. Choose the false statement in question number 1. Rewrite it to make it true.

   _____

   _____

   _____

3. You have a drum and a banjo. How are
their sounds different?

_____

- -

_____

- -

_____

4. Connect words that are related.

Pitch   Loud or soft

Volume   Share information

Communicate   High or low

5. Circle the tools you can use to
communicate with sound.

Read and answer questions 1-4.

Julio was getting ready for his concert. He had a solo! He was going to sing a song all by himself. His music teacher showed him the stage. The room was very large. He was worried his parents would not be able to hear him. His teacher told him not to worry. Julio would sing into a microphone. The microphone would make his voice sound louder. Everyone would hear his song.

1. Circle the word or words that correctly complete the sentence.

pitch   volume   percussion

The microphone would change the _____ of Julio's voice.

2. Circle the word or words that correctly complete the sentence.

Pitch   Volume   Percussion

Julio sang part of his song with a low sound. _____ is how high or low a sound is.

3. Julio's classmates played the drums and cymbals during his song. Drums and cymbals are what kind of instruments?

a. wind instruments

b. stringed instruments

c. percussion instruments

d. brass instruments

4. Julio wanted to share his concert with his aunt. She lives in another country. What devices could Julio use to communicate with his aunt?

_____

_____

_____

Evidence-Based Assessment 33

Which instrument can you use to make sound?

Phenomenon Musicians make sounds on stringed instruments, percussion instruments, and wind instruments. Musicians pluck, bang, and blow on these instruments to make sounds. Which instrument can you create to make sound?

Suggested Materials

- fishing line
- round oatmeal boxes
- pots and pans
- plastic bowls
- straws
- cardboard tubes
- shoe boxes
- clear plastic wrap
- tape
- wood spatulas
- plastic spatulas
- spoons

Design and Build It!

☐ **1.** Make a plan to design a stringed instrument, a percussion instrument, or a wind instrument.

☐ **2.** Decide which materials you will use to design your instrument.

Engineering Practice

Scientists make a plan before they investigate.

☐ **3.** Show your plan to your teacher.

☐ **4.** Draw your instrument.

☐ **5.** Build your instrument.

☐ **6.** Play a song with your instrument.

Evaluate Your Design

7. Explain how your instrument works to a partner.

8. Explain how can you improve your instrument?

Light

Lesson 1 Observe Light

Lesson 2 Light and Matter

Lesson 3 Uses of Light

Next Generation Science Standards

1-PS4-2 Make observations to construct an evidence-based account that objects can be seen only when illuminated.

1-PS4-3 Plan and conduct an investigation to determine the effect of placing objects made with different materials in the path of a beam of light.

1-PS4-4 Use tools and materials to design and build a device that uses light or sound to solve the problem of communicating over a distance.

K-2-ETS1-1 Ask questions, make observations, and gather information about a situation people want to change to define a simple problem that can be solved through the development of a new or improved object or tool.

The Essential Question How can I use light?

Show What You Know

Look at the photo.
How are the lights used?

STEM Help Send a Message

How can you use light to send a message?

Phenomenon Hi! My name is Mr. Green. I am a game designer. I design and test how games look and work.

I need your help to send messages using light in a laser tag game. Players will use light to tell the team when to stop or go. Players can show when the other team is nearby. You will make a guide of secret codes. The path shows the Quest activities you will complete. Check off your progress each time you complete an activity with a QUEST CHECK ✓ OFF .

Quest Check-In 1

Lesson 1 ■

Think of a light source that can be used to share a message.

Next Generation Science Standards

1-PS4-3 Plan and conduct an investigation to determine the effect of placing objects made with different materials in the path of a beam of light.

1-PS4-4 Use tools and materials to design and build a device that uses light or sound to solve the problem of communicating over a distance.

K-2-ETS1-1 Ask questions, make observations, and gather information about a situation people want to change to define a simple problem that can be solved through the development of a new or improved object or tool.

Quest Check-In 2

Lesson 2 ●

Identify how mirrors and paper can help you send a message with light.

Quest Check-In Lab 3

Lesson 3 ◆

Use what you have learned about light. Design a way to communicate with light.

Quest Findings

Complete the Quest! Draw and write a guide of codes. Describe how you share your messages.

What do you need to see objects?

Eye doctors use tests to find how well a person can see. How can you find out what allows a person to see?

Procedure

Materials

- box with a lid and a pin hole in one side
- crayon
- small toy
- glow in the dark sticker
- stone

☐ **1.** Do a test. View objects through the pin hole in the box with the lid on.

☐ **2.** How can you better view the objects? Test your idea. Record your observations.

Science Practice

You **use evidence** to support your ideas.

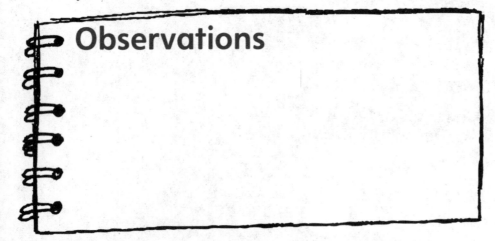

Observations

Analyze and Interpret Data

3. Use Evidence Tell what causes you to be able to see some objects and not see other objects.

Cause and Effect

A game designer may make a video game. Lights can be used in the game. Read about how light can be used.

A cause makes something happen.

An effect is the result.

Win the Game

You play a video game. You try to get a high score. When you score a point, a red light flashes. The high score wins!

☑ **Reading Check** **Cause and Effect**

What happens when you score in this video game? Underline the cause. Circle the effect.

Observe Light

▶ VIDEO

Watch a video about observing light.

Vocabulary

light

shadow

I can observe that light is needed to see objects.

I can identify objects that give off light.

1-PS4-2, 1-PS4-3

Jumpstart Discovery!

Place a piece of paper on your desk. Hold your hand out in front of you above the paper. What do you see below your hand on the paper?

What happens when an object blocks light?

Astronomers observe when objects in space block light. How can you test what happens to an object when it is placed in front of a light?

Materials
- flashlight
- toy
- white poster board

Procedure

Science Practice

You **investigate** to answer a science question.

☐ **1.** Use all of the materials to **investigate** what happens when an object blocks light.

☐ **2.** Plan a test. Include how an object looks with the light close and far. Show it to your teacher. Make observations. Draw your observations.

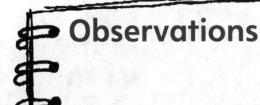

Observations

Analyze and Interpret Data

3. Tell what happens when the light is close and when the light is far.

Light and Darkness

Light is what allows you to see things. Light allows you to see people. The light from a campfire lets you to see the campsite.

Without light, you cannot see. Darkness is when there is no light. You turn on a light in a dark room to see objects. Cars use lights so drivers can see the road.

INTERACTIVITY

Complete an activity to show how light allows you to see things.

Identify Look at the picture. Circle objects that can be seen easily. Draw arrows that point to objects that are hard to see.

Where Light Comes From

Some objects give off their own light.
The sun gives off light. A lamp gives off
light. You see objects that do not give
light when light shines on them.

☑ Reading Check Cause and Effect

Underline the effect of light shining
on an object.

Quest Connection

What besides the sun and
a lamp gives off light?

campfire

Shadows

Light travels in a straight line. Some objects can block light. A **shadow** is a dark shape. It is made when light is blocked. A shadow has the same shape as whatever is blocking the light but can be a different size.

Identify Tell how a shadow is made.

shadows

Give off Light

You want to use light to send a message. Your team will see the message. What objects give off light? How can you use the objects to send a message? How will others see the light?

Identify Place an X on the light you would use to send your message.

Explain How could you send a signal with the object you chose?

_____

- -

_____

_____

- -

_____

Compare Tell why this object is better than another one for sending a message.

▶ VIDEO

Watch a video about light and matter.

Lesson 2

Light and Matter

Vocabulary

matter
opaque
transparent
translucent
reflect

I can describe how light interacts with different materials.

1-PS4-3

Jumpstart Discovery!

Hold your hand over your open eyes and look at a light. Tell what you see. Hold a piece of white paper over your eyes and look at the light. Tell what you see.

How do materials affect light?

Light engineers set stage lighting. What happens when light hits different materials?

Materials
- flashlight
- clear plastic
- waxed paper
- cardboard

Procedure

☐ 1. **Plan an investigation** to answer the title question. Show your teacher.

☐ 2. Test each material. Record what you see.

Science Practice

You **plan an investigation** to answer a science question.

Materials	Observations
cardboard	
plastic	
waxed paper	

Analyze and Interpret Data

3. **Infer** Tell which material you would use to cover a window to make a room dark. Explain why.

Blocked Light

Anything that takes up space is **matter**. A tree is made of matter. A window is made of matter. You are made of matter.

Matter that blocks all light is **opaque**. You cannot see through something opaque. A tree blocks all light. You block all light. Opaque matter makes shadows.

List Say classroom objects that are opaque.

Light Goes Through

Matter that lets almost all light through is **transparent**. Air lets light through. Water lets light through. Clear glass can let light through.

Translucent matter blocks some light. A lamp shade blocks some light. Colored glass can block some light.

Identify Look at the playground. Circle an object that is opaque. Draw an X on an object that is transparent. Draw a box around an object that is translucent.

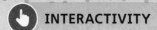

INTERACTIVITY

Complete an activity to choose materials that block light or let light shine through.

Light Bounces Off

Light can bounce off matter. Matter **reflects** light when the light bounces off it.

Smooth and shiny objects reflect light. Mirrors reflect light. Foil reflects light.

Light travels in straight lines. It travels in a straight line to the mirror. Light hits the mirror. It changes direction. Then it travels in another straight line away from the mirror. Light changes direction when it reflects.

☑ **Reading Check** **Cause and Effect**
What happens to light when it reflects?

_____

_____

_____

Materials That Reflect

Materials that reflect light can be opaque. They can also be transparent or translucent.

Some water can reflect a lot of light. Some metal and some glass reflect a lot of light too.

Light shines on a lake. The light bounces off the lake. The water reflects light. You see the trees and sky on the lake.

Cause and Effect
Read about the lake. What causes you to see the trees and sky on the lake? Underline the cause.

Quest Connection

How can you use materials that reflect light to send a message?

Materials for a Light Signal

How can you use different materials to make a signal with light? How can you keep it a secret?

You will use light to send messages for your laser tag game. You will also use different materials.

Describe How can you use mirrors, colored glass, and light to send a message?

_____

_____

_____

_____

How can you see what is behind you?

Phenomenon Imagine you are a spy. You are watching a movie. You are in the front row.

A woman is bringing you a secret note. How can you know when she is there? You will be caught if you turn around.

TOP SECRET

Apply Concepts What object can you use to see the back of the theater? Tell how you would use the object.

_____
_____
_____

7

µEngineer It! Define STEM

Windshield Safety

INTERACTIVITY

Go online to learn about designing a boat with different materials.

Phenomenon Cars must be designed for safety. Seat belts help people stay in place. Airbags protect people in a crash.

Car safety engineers design safety features. They test the features.

dirty windshield

Define It

You are a car safety engineer. You are asked to test windshield safety.

☐ Ask questions about windshield safety.

_____

- - - - - - - - - - - - - - - - - - - -

_____

☐ State safety concerns of dirty windshields.

_____

- - - - - - - - - - - - - - - - - - - -

_____

☐ Define a windshield safety problem you will try to fix.

_____

- - - - - - - - - - - - - - - - - - - -

_____

☐ Describe a possible solution to the problem.

_____

- - - - - - - - - - - - - - - - - - - -

_____

Uses of Light

▶ **VIDEO**

Watch a video about uses of light.

Vocabulary

communicate

I can explain how people use light.

I can identify how people use light to communicate with others who are far away.

1-PS4-3, 1-PS4-4, K-2-ETS1-1

Jumpstart Discovery!

Why are the headlights on the car turned on? What would happen if the car did not have headlights?

How can you use light to see?

Dentists use mirrors to see the teeth in the back of your mouth. How can you use a mirror to help you see around a corner?

Materials
- 2 mirrors
- small toy
- cardboard

Procedure

Science Practice

You **use evidence** to explain why something happens.

☐ **1.** Use the cardboard to build a maze with two turns. Place the toy at the end of the maze.

☐ **2.** Plan a way to see the toy from the start of the maze. Show your plan to your teacher.

Analyze and Interpret Data

3. Use evidence from your investigation. How did you use light?

_____

_____

_____

_____

Light and Mood

Theaters use light for mood. Mood makes you feel a certain way.

A theater uses bright yellow lights. This can make you feel happy.

A theater uses dark purple lights. This can make you feel scared.

When is bright light used? Bright light helps when reading. Bright light helps you see when writing.

Engineering Practice ▸ Toolbox

Design Solutions You will sing at a talent show. Design stage lights. Design lights for the audience. Share your design with a classmate.

Analyze Underline evidence of why a library has bright lights.

INTERACTIVITY

Complete an activity on the uses of light.

Communciate with Light

Lights can be used to communicate. You **communicate** when you share a message. Lights tell you what to do. A lit-up sign can tell you where to go. A lit-up sign can tell you when a store is open.

Lights keep you safe. Lights keep you from tripping. Lights warn you of danger.

Infer What is the message of the lights on an ambulance? Write a caption for the photo that gives the message.

_____

_____

Uses of Light

Light lets you see.
Lights make a mood.
Lights keep you safe.
Lights give you directions.

Visual Literacy

Find the lights with a message. Circle the pictures of lights that give a message.

SAN CLEMENTE

Quest Connection

Tell all the ways you can use light in a laser tag game.

How can **you** send secret messages?

A game designer uses light to communicate. You will make secret codes to send messages. One message warns when someone from the other team is nearby. Another message says stop. A third message says go. How can you use light to send messages?

Materials
• flashlight

Suggested Materials
• colored filters
• mirrors
• cardboard box

Engineering Practice

You **design a solution** to communicate a message.

Design and Test

☐ **1. Design a solution** to communicate messages with light. Choose which materials to use. Write or draw your codes. Show the codes to your teacher.

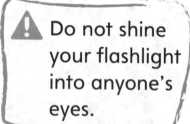

⚠ Do not shine your flashlight into anyone's eyes.

☐ **2.** Test your codes. See if another group can identify the code.

☐ **3.** Make changes to your codes if needed.

☐ **4.** Test your codes again.

Evaluate Your Design

5. Assess Which codes worked well? How else could you keep your codes a secret?

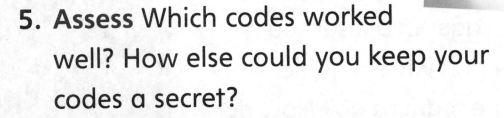

_____

_____

_____

_____

6. Identify Use what you learned about light. Describe a new way to communicate with light.

_____

_____

_____

_____

INTERACTIVITY

Apply what you learned in the Quest.

STEM

Help Send a Message

How was light used to send a secret message?

Show What You Found

Phenomenon Share your plan for sending messages in a laser tag game. Draw and write a guide. How do you tell the team to go? How do you tell the team to stop? How do you tell when others are close? Describe how to keep the messages a secret.

Career Connection

Game Designer

Game designers plan, build, and test games. They solve problems so the game will work. They may design board games. They may design video games.

Video game designers use lights. They use lights for rewards. They use light to show a path. They also use lights to show time left.

How would you use lights in a video game?

_____

_____

_____

_____

SHIP NAME

NEW GAME

LOAD GAME

OPTIONS

EXIT GAME

START BONUS   CHOOSE OPTION ▼

GENERATE RANDOM   START GAME

The Essential Question **How can I use light?**

Show What You Learned
Tell a partner how you use light.

1. What do you need to see all objects?

   a. mirrors

   b. light

   c. matter

   d. shadows

2. Why are there shadows?

3. Look at the pictures. Circle the transparent object. Put a check mark on the translucent object. Put an X over the opaque object.

4. Give three examples of light that sends a message.

_____

_____

_____

Read and answer questions 1–4.

Krystal is camping in the woods. During lunch, she cannot finish her sandwich. She wants to save it for later. She wraps it in foil. She puts the sandwich in a bin.

After dark, Krystal wants to finish her sandwich. There are three bins. She uses her flashlight to look in one bin. Her sandwich is not there. She shines the flashlight into the next bin. Light reflects back. She has found her sandwich.

1. Why did Krystal use a flashlight to look for her sandwich?

   a. so light could shine through the bin

   b. so there would be a shadow

   c. so she could see the sandwich

   d. so the sandwich would be transparent

2. Why did light reflect off the foil?

    a. The foil is translucent.

    b. The foil gives off light.

    c. The foil is transparent.

    d. The foil is smooth and shiny.

3. Circle the word that correctly completes the sentence.

Krystal had to open the lid to see in the bin because the bin is _____.

opaque	transparent	translucent	reflective

4. Would Krystal need to use the flashlight to find her sandwich during the day? Why or why not?

_____

_____

_____

_____

_____

_____

How can I change a transparent material?

Phenomenon Light engineers test how light shines through materials. How can you change a transparent material so that less light gets through?

Materials
- flashlight
- 1/2 cup water in a clear plastic cup
- 1 cup of milk

Procedure

☐ **1.** Use all of the materials. Make a plan to change a material from transparent to translucent to opaque.

☐ **2.** Show your plan to your teacher. Follow your plan. Record your observations.

Science Practice

You **use evidence** to support your ideas.

⚠ **Do not taste.**

Observations

Materials	Did light get through? Yes, No, or Some	Opaque, Transparent, or Translucent

Analyze and Interpret Data

3. **Use Evidence** Tell how you identified when transparent material became translucent or opaque.

4. **Identify** Tell how you can change another object from transparent to translucent or opaque.

Sky and Earth

1-ESS1-1 Use observations of the sun, moon, and stars to describe patterns that can be predicted.

1-ESS1-2 Make observations at different times of year to relate the amount of daylight to the time of year.

K-2-ETS1-1 Ask questions, make observations, and gather information about a situation people want to change to define a simple problem that can be solved through the development of a new or improved object or tool.

K-2-ETS1-2 Develop a simple sketch, drawing, or physical model to illustrate how the shape of an object helps it function as needed to solve a given problem.

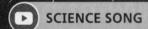

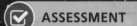

The Essential Question

What objects are in the sky, and how do they move?

Show What You Know

What do people see in the sky when they look through a telescope? How does a telescope change how objects in the sky look? Tell a partner.

Sky Watchers

What patterns can you see in the sky?

Phenomenon Hi! My name is Ms. Collins. I am a space scientist. I heard some students talking about the night sky. One student said, "I saw a round moon. There were too many stars to count!" Another student said, "I saw a moon that looked like a smile. There were only a few stars!" A third student said, "I can't see the moon on some nights!"

All the students were right! How can that be? Help me explain patterns in the sky to the students. The path shows the Quest activities you will complete as you work through the topic. Check off your progress each time you complete an activity with a

QUEST CHECK ✓ **OFF** .

1-ESS1-1 Use observations of the sun, moon, and stars to describe patterns that can be predicted.

VIDEO

Watch a video about a space scientist.

Quest Check-In Lab 3

Lesson 3 ◆

Model how Earth moves.

Quest Check-In 2

Lesson 2 ○

Tell which picture shows what you see through a telescope.

Quest Check-In 1

Lesson 1 ■

Tell how stars look in the sky.

Quest Findings

Complete the Quest! Find a fun way to show patterns in the sky.

uConnect Lab

Which way will it point?

Space scientists need to study forces. What tools can you use to study one of these forces?

Procedure

Materials
- paper clip
- string
- pencil
- table

☐ 1. Find a way to use the materials to make the paper clip hang down.

☐ 2. Try to make the paper clip hang on its side. Predict what you think will happen.

Science Practice

You **ask questions** to find out more about phenomena.

_____

_____

_____

_____

Analyze and Interpret Data

3. Did what you see support your prediction? Why or why not?

_____

_____

4. What might happen if you move the paper clip off the desk with nothing to hold it up?

_____

_____

Picture Clues

Space scientists study pictures of space to find patterns. What can you learn by studying a picture?

Pictures are like clues. They can help you figure out what you are reading. They can help you learn more about the text. Read the text below, then look at the picture.

GAME
Practice what you learn with the Mini Games.

Seeing Earth

Look out the window. Can you see all of Earth? We cannot see all of Earth from one place. Spacecraft move around Earth. They can take pictures of Earth from space. The pictures help us see all of Earth.

☑**Reading Check** **Picture Clues** Tell what the picture shows. Tell one thing you learned from this picture.

Observe the Sky

 VIDEO

Watch a video about stars.

Vocabulary

star

sun

gravity

I can describe the sun, the moon, and the stars.

1-ESS1-1

Jumpstart Discovery!

What do you see in the day sky? Draw it on a sheet of paper. Then draw what you see in the night sky. Tell how your drawings are alike and different.

HANDS-ON LAB

1-ESS1-1, SEP.2, SEP.3, SEP.4

Why is it hard to see stars during the day?

On clear nights, you can see many stars in the sky. Why can we only see the sun during the day?

Material
• flashlight

Science Practice
You **use models** to show what something is like in real life.

Procedure

☐ **1.** Make a plan to **model** a star in the night sky and day sky. Use the flashlight.

☐ **2.** Show your plan to your teacher before you start.

☐ **3.** Record your observations.

night	**day**

Analyze and Interpret Data

4. Explain Why can you see the sun but no other stars during the day?

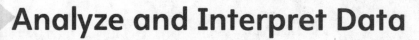

Star Light, Star Bright

A **star** is a big ball of hot gas. Stars look small because they are far away from us.

Stars are seen at night. You cannot see most stars in the day.

Have you ever tried to count all the stars in the sky? There are too many stars to count!

Draw Conclusions Look at the night sky. Tell a partner how easy it is to count the stars. Tell how the stars are scattered all over the sky.

The Sun, Our Star

You can see only one star in the day.
The sun is a star.

The **sun** is the closest star to Earth.
This is why it looks bigger and brighter
than other stars. We cannot live
without heat and light from the sun.

The sun can also harm living things.
It can give you a sunburn.

Identify Underline one way the sun is
helpful. Circle one way the sun is harmful.

Quest Connection

When can you see many
stars? When can you only see
the sun? Describe the pattern
to a partner.

Gravity and the Moon

Gravity is a force, like a pull. It pulls objects toward one another. Gravity pulls objects to the center of Earth. It makes a ball fall to the ground. It keeps you from floating into space.

The moon is the closest large object to Earth in space. Gravity keeps the moon close to Earth.

Explain Nothing is touching these paper planes. Draw an arrow to show how Earth's gravity will affect them. Tell a partner why this will happen. Test paper planes in your class to see if you were correct.

Stars in the Sky

Look at the pictures.

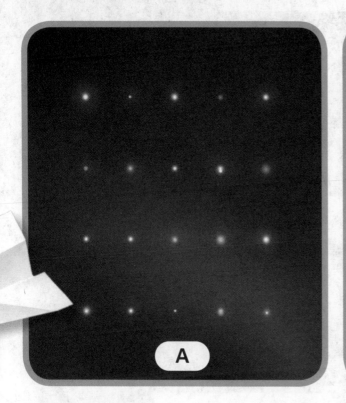

A

B

1. Circle the picture that shows the way stars appear in the sky.

2. Why did you choose this picture?

_____

_____

_____

Patterns in the Sky

Earth's rotation.

Vocabulary

rotation

sunrise

sunset

moon phase

I can tell what causes day and night and moon phases.

_____

1-ESS1-1, 1-ESS1-2, K-2-ETS1-2

Jumpstart Discovery!

How many different shapes of the moon have you seen? Draw the shapes on a sheet of paper. Cut out the shapes. Put the shapes on a night sky poster.

HANDS-ON LAB

1-ESS1-1, SEP.3, SEP.8

How can you observe sun patterns?

Space scientists study the sun during the day. What patterns can you see in the day sky?

Science Practice

You **plan and carry out investigations** to explain phenomena.

Procedure

☐ **1.** Make a plan to observe sun patterns throughout the day.

☐ **2.** Show your plan to your teacher.

☐ **3.** Make your observations. Draw them.

 Never look directly at the sun.

Analyze and Interpret Data

4. Explain How does the sun seem to move in a pattern during the day?

_____

_____

Earth Spins

Earth spins in space. It makes one spin every 24 hours. This motion is called **rotation**.

Rotation causes day and night. As Earth spins, one half of Earth faces the sun. It is daytime there.

The other half of Earth faces away from the sun. It is nighttime there.

sunrise

Identify Make a small **X** on the picture of Earth. Tell whether it is day or night at that place.

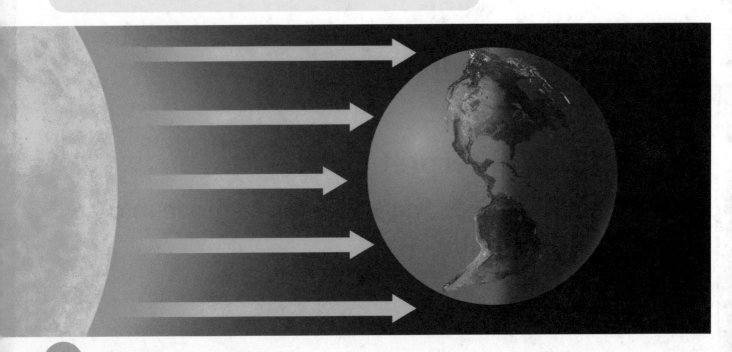

Sunrise, Sunset

Sunrise is a pattern that happens when the sun seems to rise in the morning. Then the sun seems to move across the sky. It is high in the sky around noon.

Sunset is a pattern that happens when the sun seems to set in the evening. The sun is not moving. The rotation of Earth makes the sun seem to move.

sunset

Explain What makes the sun seem to move? Fill in the box.

Cause		Effect
	▶	The sun seems to move.

Moon Motions and Phases

The moon moves in a path around Earth. It takes the moon a little less than a month to go around Earth. The moon spins just like Earth does.

The sun shines on the moon. This makes the moon bright at night.

The moon seems to change shape. As the moon moves around Earth, the amount of sun that shines on it changes. The changing shapes of the moon are called **moon phases**.

Math ▸ Toolbox

Use Tools Plan a way to use a tool to observe the shapes of the moon in the sky. Write or draw what you see. What kinds of shapes does the moon appear to make?

A Closer View

INTERACTIVITY

Go online to explore patterns in the night sky.

Would you like to see the moon or stars up close? A telescope is a tool that makes things look bigger.

You can use a telescope to see the sky. The moon looks bigger. You can see more stars in the sky.

Never look at the sun with this tool. You could hurt your eyes.

☑ **Reading Check** **Picture Clues**
How do you use a telescope? Look at the picture for clues.

Quest Connection

What can space scientists learn by using telescopes to look at the sky? Tell a partner.

Moon Patterns

Look at the pictures.
They show the full moon.

Think about the phases of the moon. What do they tell you about how the moon moves around Earth?

Put a small **X** on the full moon you would see through a telescope. What details can you see on this full moon that you cannot see on the other? Why?

_____

- -

_____

Use a Calendar

The moon goes through phases. The moon takes **29** days to go through all its phases. You can predict the next full moon.

Sun	Mon	Tue	Wed	Thu	Fri	Sat
				1	2	3
4	5	6	7	8	9	10
11	12	13	14	15	16	17
18	19	20	21	22	23	24
25	26	27	28	29	30	31

Find the full moon. What is the date of the full moon? Predict the date of the next full moon.

Draw the next full moon on the calendar.

Daylight Changes and Seasons

 VIDEO

Watch a video to learn about patterns of daylight in different seasons.

 INTERACTIVITY

Go online to learn more about the seasons.

Vocabulary

season

I can explain why days have different lengths during different seasons.

1-ESS1-2

Jumpstart Discovery!

Act out something you like to do in your favorite season. Have a partner guess your favorite season.

How does the sun cause seasons?

In many places, seasons change. How can you model seasons?

Materials

- balloon
- marker
- light source

Procedure

☐ 1. Use the materials to **model** how sunlight hits Earth. Make a plan to collect data at three spots on your model Earth.

☐ 2. Show your plan to your teacher.

☐ 3. Think of a way to change how light hits your model of Earth as it moves around the model sun. Record your observations.

Science Practice

You **use models** to show what something is like in real life.

Analyze and Interpret Data

4. **Explain** What happened to light on your model of Earth? Tell a partner.

Seasons

Earth moves around the sun. Earth makes one path around the sun in 365 days.

As Earth moves, sunlight hits parts of Earth differently. These patterns can be predicted. This causes seasons. **Seasons** are summer, fall, winter, and spring.

Visual Literacy

Which season are you having now? Circle the picture.

Quest Connection

What patterns in the amount of daylight do you observe at different times of the year?

In summer, your part of Earth gets a lot of sunshine. Daylight hours are long. Summer is warm.

In fall, your part of Earth gets a little less sunshine. Daylight hours get shorter. Fall is cool.

In spring, your part of Earth begins to get more sunshine. Daylight hours get longer. Spring is cool.

In winter, your part of Earth gets the least amount of sunshine. Daylight hours are short. Winter is cold. Draw something you see in winter.

How can you model the motions of Earth?

Materials
- construction paper
- flashlight
- drawing materials

Earth spins once every day. It moves around the sun in one year. How can you model these motions? How can you show what the motions cause?

Science Practice

You **use models** to learn how objects move.

Procedure

☐ **1.** In your group, decide who will be the models for different objects in the sky.

☐ **2.** Plan how your models will work.

☐ **3.** Show your teacher your plan.

☐ **4.** **Model** one pattern caused by the rotation of Earth. Explain how your model works.

_____

_____

_____

_____

Analyze and Interpret Data

5. Describe What patterns did you model?

_____

_____

_____

6. Connect How could you model seasons?

_____

_____

_____

7. Draw Conclusions How do movements
of Earth change how we live?

_____

_____

_____

Design a Code

VIDEO

Watch a video about how Earth revolves around the sun.

Phenomenon Earth takes one year to move around the sun. There are 12 months in a year. How can you make a code to tell where Earth is each month?

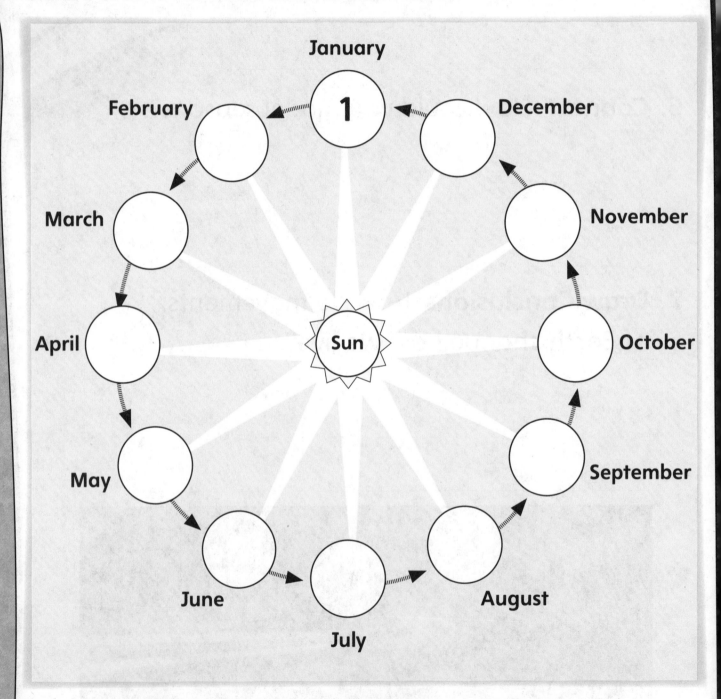

Design It

The picture shows Earth moving around the sun. Position 1 is Earth in January. Each circle stands for a different month.

☐ **1.** Design a code that tells about Earth's position around the sun each month.

☐ **2.** Write four months of your code here.

_____   _____

_____   _____

_____   _____

☐ **3.** Share your code. Tell how it works.

_____

_____

_____

☐ **4.** See if your code works. Use a code number to describe the position of Earth. Your partner should tell you what month it is.

INTERACTIVITY

Go online for ideas for your play about sky patterns.

Sky Watchers

What patterns can you see in the sky?

Phenomenon Look back through the pages. How many patterns can you find? Draw a pattern you see.

Show What You Found

Work in a group. Write a play that shows patterns in the sky. You can use drawings in your play. You can use photos. People can be the sun, the moon, the stars, and Earth. Use your play to describe and predict patterns based on your observations of the sun, moon, and stars.

Space Scientist

Space scientists study objects in space. They observe the sun and moon. They study Earth, too. Space scientists use telescopes. They study pictures taken by spacecraft.

Some space scientists travel in space. They live in spacecraft that move around Earth. Do you see the floating objects in the top image? There is very little gravity in space. The space scientists float, too.

What object in the sky would you like to study?

_____

- -

_____

What objects are in the sky, and how do they move?

Show What You Learned

Tell a partner what you learned about how objects in the sky move.

1. Which sentence describes stars?

   a. Stars are close to Earth.

   b. Stars give off light and heat.

   c. We see stars during the day.

   d. Stars are spaced evenly in the sky.

2. What does the picture show?

   a. a phase of the moon

   b. the rotation of Earth

   c. a cause of seasons

   d. the rising of the sun

3. How do hours of daylight change with the seasons? Use the word bank to fill in the table.

| winter | more | fewer | summer |

Season	Hours of Daylight

4. Mia counted the hours of daylight on a spring day. She did the same thing on a fall day. What did she notice?

_____

_____

_____

_____

_____

_____

Read this scenario and answer the questions.

Kate made a model of patterns in the sky. She used a ball and a lamp in her model. She made the ball spin in front of the lamp. Then she moved the ball in a circle around the lamp. Sean made a video of the two types of motion. He wrote a script to tell about the movement of the model.

1. What things did Kate model?
   a. The ball was Earth. The lamp was the sun.
   b. The ball was the moon. The lamp was a star.
   c. The ball was a star. The lamp was Earth.
   d. The ball was the sun. The lamp was the moon.

2. What did Kate model when she made the ball spin?

_____

- -

_____

3. What did Sean's script say when the ball spun in front of the lamp?

a. Earth's rotation causes seasons.

b. The moon's rotation causes moon phases.

c. Earth's rotation causes day and night.

d. The moon's path around the sun causes sunrise.

4. What did Kate model when she moved the ball around the lamp?

_____

_____

_____

_____

5. What did Sean's script say to describe the ball moving around the lamp?

a. The moon's rotation causes moon phases.

b. The moon's path around Earth causes sunset.

c. Earth's rotation causes day and night.

d. Earth's path around the sun causes seasons.

How do shadows change?

Materials
- wood stick
- ruler

Phenomenon Earth's movement causes shadows from the sun in patterns that can be predicted. What tools can you use to observe these patterns?

Science Practice

You **plan investigations** to explain phenomena.

Procedure

☐ **1.** Predict if a shadow stays the same during the day.

☐ **2.** Make a plan to test your prediction. Use all the materials. Remember to take measurements.

☐ **3.** Show your plan to your teacher before you begin.

☐ **4.** Make **your observations**.

Observations

	Length of shadow	How the pattern changed
Observation 1		
Observation 2		
Observation 3		

Analyze and Interpret Data

5. Interpret What happened to the shadow?

_____

_____

_____

_____

6. Explain What pattern do your observations show?

_____

_____

_____

_____

Weather and Seasons

Lesson 1 Types of Weather

Lesson 2 Weather Changes and Seasons

Next Generation Science Standards
1-ESS1-2 Make observations at different times of year to relate the amount of daylight to the time of year. **K-2-ETS1-2** Develop a simple sketch, drawing, or physical model to illustrate how the shape of an object helps it function as needed to solve a given problem.

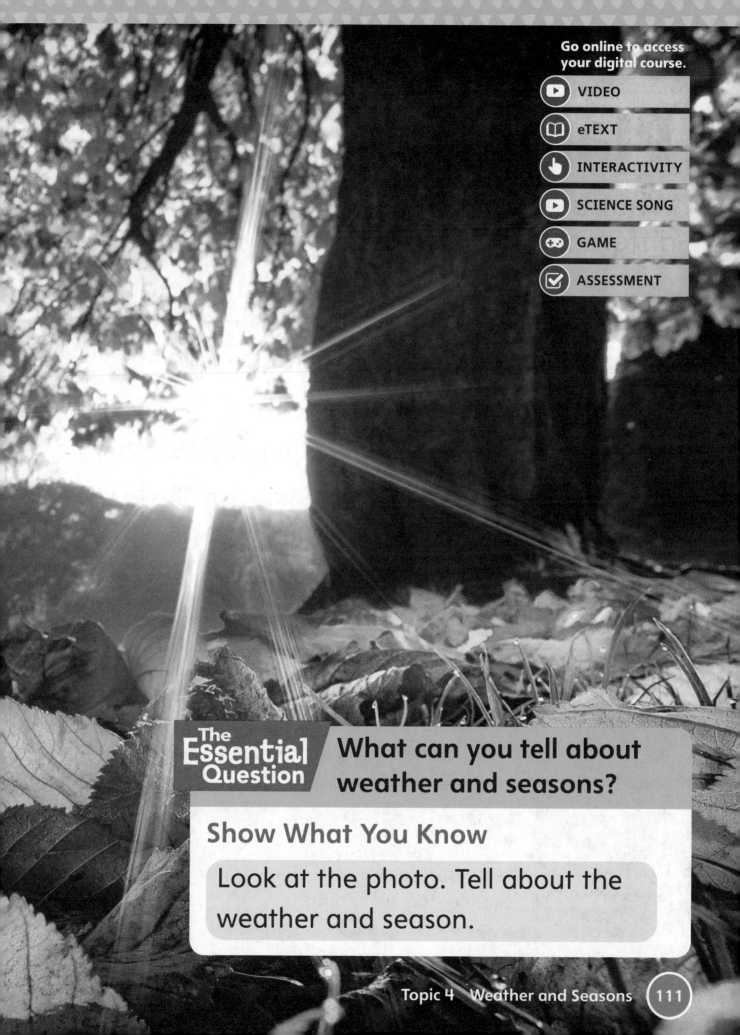

Go online to access
your digital course.

▶ VIDEO

📖 eTEXT

👆 INTERACTIVITY

▶ SCIENCE SONG

🎮 GAME

☑ ASSESSMENT

The Essential Question What can you tell about weather and seasons?

Show What You Know

Look at the photo. Tell about the weather and season.

Plan a Trip!

What are the best seasons for different activities?

Phenomenon Hi! I am Mr. Bloomfield. I am a meteorologist. I predict and explain weather.

I need your help to make a trip guide. Weather affects what you can do on a trip. The guide will show families the best place and time of year for their trip. The path shows the Quest activities you will complete as you work through the topic. Check off your progress each time you complete an activity with a **QUEST CHECK ✓ OFF** .

Quest Check-In 1

Lesson 1
Identify the best temperatures for ice skating and swimming.

Next Generation Science Standards
1-ESS1-2 Develop a simple sketch, drawing, or physical model to illustrate how the shape of an object helps it function as needed to solve a given problem

Quest Findings

Complete the Quest! Choose
activities for a family trip.
Identify the best time and
place for these activities. Find
a creative way to make your
trip guide.

Quest Check-In Lab 2

Lesson 2

Use what you have learned
about daylight in different
seasons. Observe patterns
in sunrise and sunset data
for each season.

What is it like (outside) today?

Many types of scientists work outside. They must check the weather every day. How can you check the weather today?

Procedure

☐ **1.** Write a question you want to **ask** about the weather.

_____

_____

_____

☐ **2.** Use your senses to observe the weather. Record your observations.

Analyze and Interpret Data

3. How do your observations answer your question? Tell a partner.

 Do not look directly at the sun.

Observations

Sequence

Meteorologists study and predict the weather. Read about how rain clouds form.

Sequence is the order in which things happen. A sequence uses words such as "first," "next," "then," and "last."

🎮 **Game**

Practice what you learn with the Mini Games.

Rain Clouds Form

First, warm air rises. Second, the air starts to cool. Then some gas changes into water. Next, many small drops of water gather in clouds. Then the rain falls. The water goes into the ground, lakes, and rivers. The sun warms the water. Some of the water turns into gas. Last, the gas goes into the sky and forms clouds. Then it rains again.

☑ **Reading Check** **Sequence** Write what happens after warm air rises and starts to cool.

_____

_____

Types of Weather

▶ **VIDEO**

Watch a video about how to use weather tools.

Vocabulary

weather
thermometer
rain gauge
anemometer
tornado
blizzard

I can observe and measure weather.

K-2-ETS1-2

Jumpstart Discovery!

What is your favorite kind of weather? Take a class vote. Talk about why you like your favorite kind of weather.

Which way is the wind blowing?

Meteorologists report which way wind blows. How can you tell which way the wind blows?

Design and Build

☐ 1. Use all of the materials. Draw your wind vane design on a piece of paper. Show your design to your teacher.

☐ 2. Build your wind vane.

☐ 3. Use your wind vane to find the direction of the wind. **Collect data**.

Materials

• unsharpened pencil
• pen cap
• plastic straw
• construction paper
• scissors
• plastic cup with lid
• pebbles
• marker
• tape

Engineering Practice

You **collect data** to help you answer a question.

 Be careful using scissors.

Evaluate Your Design

4. **Compare** Share data with a partner. Tell how the data are alike or different.

Weather

When you went outside this morning, what did you see? What did you feel? **Weather** is how it feels and looks outside.

Sometimes it is sunny outside. Other times, clouds cover the sky. The wind is gentle on some days. It is strong on other days. Some days are warm, and other days are cool or cold. A day might include rain, snow, or fog.

Illustrate Draw a picture of what the weather looks like today.

Temperature

Temperature is how hot or cold something is. A **thermometer** is a tool that measures temperature. Scientists use thermometers to study weather.

Measure Read the thermometer in the image. What temperature does it show?

Quest Connection

Tell what you think the best weather is for flying a kite.

Wind

Wind is the movement of air. Scientists use wind vanes to observe wind direction. An **anemometer** measures how fast the wind moves.

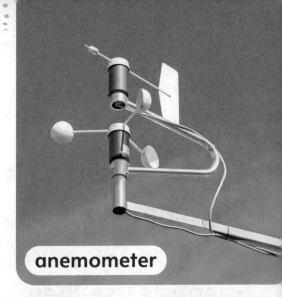
anemometer

Rain and Snow

Water falls as rain when it is warm. Scientists use a tool called a **rain gauge** to measure how much rain has fallen.

Water freezes at 0 °Celsius (32 °Fahrenheit) or below. Water falls as snow at those cold temperatures.

rain gauge

Math ▸ Toolbox

Interpret Data Look at the chart. On how many days did it rain? On how many days was it dry? How many more dry days were there than rainy days?

Day of the Week	Rain	No Rain
Monday		X
Tuesday		X
Wednesday	X	
Thursday		X
Friday	X	

Storms

Heavy rain or snow is a storm. A thunderstorm has rain, lightning, and thunder. A **tornado** is a storm with high winds. The winds twist in a funnel shape. Tornadoes form during some thunderstorms. Tornadoes can destroy buildings.

A **blizzard** is a storm with high winds and snow. Blizzards can block roads. Blizzards can knock down power lines.

☑ **Reading Check** **Sequence**
Does a thunderstorm or a tornado come first? Tell a partner.

tornado

blizzard

Quest Check-In

Hot and Cold

Sometimes it is hot. Sometimes it is cold. Different days have different temperatures.

Identify Find the temperature that would be best for ice skating outside. Circle that thermometer.

Identify Find the temperature that would be best for swimming outside. Draw an X on that thermometer.

QUEST CHECK ✓ OFF

EXTREME science

Winter Storm Jonas

Winter Storm Jonas happened in the northeast United States in January 2016. The storm lasted for three days. Snow fell in 26 states. Some parts of the country got 51 cm of snow. Some got 76 cm of snow. New York, New Jersey, Pennsylvania, Maryland, Virginia, and West Virginia had some of the most snow.

Illustrate Draw a picture of what you think a winter storm looks like.

VIDEO

Watch a video about how engineers design tools.

Design a Cooler!

Phenomenon Engineers make objects that people use. One of those objects is a cooler. A cooler keeps food and drinks cool when it is hot outside. Would you like to help an engineer design a cooler?

Design It

You want to take cold drinks and fruit to a beach. You do not have a cooler. You look around your home. What can you use to keep the drinks and fruit cold?

☐ List materials you could use to make your cooler.

_____

_____

_____

_____

_____

_____

☐ Draw a design of the cooler in the space below.

☐ Compare your materials and design with another student's. How are they alike? How are they different?

_____

_____

_____

_____

Weather Changes and Seasons

▶ **VIDEO**

Watch a video about weather and seasons.

Vocabulary

shelter

I can describe how weather changes from day to day.

I can describe seasons.

1-ESS1-2

Jumpstart Discovery!

Look at the picture. Act out an activity you can do during this time of year. Have a partner guess the activity.

How can you make it rain?

Many storms have rain. How can you make a model of rain?

Procedure

☐ 1. Put a plate on top of the jar with hot water.

☐ 2. Put ice on the plate. Draw what you see on the bottom of the plate on the Rainmaker Sheet.

☐ 3. Tap the plate. Tell a partner what happens.

Analyze and Interpret Data

4. **Explain** Why do you think it rained in the jar? Tell a partner.

Materials
- jar
- hot tap water
- ice cubes
- plate
- Rainmaker Sheet

Science Practice

You **make a model** to study nature.

Daily Weather Changes

The weather can change from day to day. Some days it is sunny and warm. Some days it is rainy and cool. Weather can be different each day even during the same season, or time of year. There are four seasons. They are spring, summer, fall, and winter.

Identify Underline the sentence that tells the main idea of the paragraph.

INTERACTIVITY

Complete an activity that explores the four seasons.

sunny day

rainy day

Quest Connection

Look at the pictures. Circle the picture that shows the best weather for a picnic in a garden.

Sunlight and Seasons

Earth gets different amounts of sunlight during different seasons. In the spring, the sun rises early and sets late. The days get longer and warmer. In the summer, the sun rises very early. It sets very late. Summer days have the most daylight. The days are hot.

In the fall, the sun rises early and sets late again. The days get shorter and cooler. In the winter, the sun rises very late. It sets very early. Winter days have the least daylight. The days are short and cold.

Literacy ▸ Toolbox

Sequence Tell how daylight changes in each season. Start with spring and end with winter.

sunrise in winter

sunrise in summer

129

Seasonal Weather Changes

Visual Literacy Circle the picture of the season that has the most plant growth.

In the winter, it is cold. Snow may fall. Plants do not grow. Some animals go to sleep or go to warmer areas.

In the spring, it gets warmer. Plants grow. Animals have young.

In the summer, it is hot. Plants and animals grow.

In the fall, it gets cooler. Trees drop their leaves. Animals store food and make shelter. **Shelter** is a place that provides protection.

How does **the season affect the amount of** daylight?

Materials

• Sunrise and Sunset for Each Season Sheets

Meteorologists study the seasons. You can use the patterns of daylight in each season to choose activities to include in your trip guide. How can you find out whether the amount of daylight varies from season to season?

Science Practice

You **observe patterns** when you study data.

Procedure

☐ **1.** Look at the Sunrise and Sunset for Each Season Sheets. **Observe patterns** for the time of sunrise and sunset in each season.

☐ **2.** Make a plan to observe the sunset in your area for five days. Show your plan to your teacher.

3. Observe the sunset for five days. Record the time in the data table.

Observations

	Sunset Time				
Season					
Day	1	2	3	4	5
Time					

Analyze and Interpret Data

4. Compare How are your data alike or different from the data in the Sheets?

_____

_____

_____

_____

5. Explain Tell about the pattern in the data. Describe the amount of daylight at different times of year.

6. Predict Tell how the sunset will change in the week after your observations.

Plan a Trip!

What are the best seasons for different activities?

Show What You Found

Phenomenon Think about activities for a family trip. What season would be best? Research places in the United States that have good weather for the activities.

Choose a creative way to make your trip guide. You could make a video or a poster. Show the place and activities. Explain why the kind of weather is best for the activities.

QUEST CHECK ✓ OFF

Career Connection

Meteorologist

Meteorologists study and explain weather. They also predict weather.

Some meteorologists work for news programs. Others work for the government or companies. They study weather patterns.

What types of weather would you study if you were a meteorologist? Explain.

_____

_____

_____

_____

_____

The Essential Question

What can you tell about weather and seasons?

Show What You Learned

Tell a partner what you learned about weather in different seasons.

1. What do people use to measure the temperature of the air?
   a. wind vane
   b. thermometer
   c. rain gauge
   d. anemometer

2. Write how tornadoes and blizzards are alike.

   _____

   _____

   _____

   _____

   _____

3. Use the word bank to complete these sentences.

| summer   winter |

The _____ season has the most amount of daylight and the longest days.

The _____ season has the least amount of daylight and the shortest days.

4. Look at the photos. Write the season under each photo.

_____

_____

Read and answer questions 1–4.

Liza woke up very early in the morning. The sun was rising. She played outside all day. It was hot. The sun set very late. Liza heard a warning on the radio the next day. The meteorologist said a storm was moving toward Liza's town. The storm had strong winds. The winds were moving more than 50 kilometers per hour. The meteorologist said the storm was dangerous. He said the winds might turn into a funnel shape.

1. What tool did the meteorologist most likely use to measure the wind speed?

    a. thermometer

    b. wind vane

    c. rain gauge

    d. anemometer

2. What type of storm does the meteorologist think could happen?

    a. blizzard

    b. drought

    c. tornado

    d. rain storm

3. What season is it?

    a. spring

    b. summer

    c. fall

    d. winter

4. Why do you think it is that season? Explain.

_____

_____

_____

_____

_____

_____

uDemonstrate Lab

How does **weather** change in a week?

Phenomenon The weather changes from day to day. How can you measure the changes in weather?

Procedure

☐ **1.** Decide which type of weather you want to measure. **Ask** a question about that type of weather. Write it down.

_____

- - - - - - - - - - - - - - - - - -

_____

- - - - - - - - - - - - - - - - - -

_____

☐ **2.** Choose your materials. Make a plan to measure the type of weather for five days. Show your plan to your teacher.

Suggested Materials

- thermometer
- rain gauge
- wind vane
- anemometer

 Do not look directly at the sun.

Science Practice

You **ask** questions to find out more about nature.

☐ **3.** Measure the weather for five days. Record your observations.

Observations

Day	Measurement
1	
2	
3	
4	
5	

Analyze and Interpret Data

4. Tell how the weather changed over the week.

5. Tell how you can use your observations to answer your question.

Living Things

1-LS1-1 Use materials to design a solution to a human problem by mimicking how plants and/or animals use their external parts to help them survive, grow, and meet their needs.

K-2-ETS1-1 Ask questions, make observations, and gather information about a situation people want to change to define a simple problem that can be solved through the development of a new or improved object or tool.

K-2-ETS1-2 Develop a simple sketch, drawing, or physical model to illustrate how the shape of an object helps it function as needed to solve a given problem.

K-2-ETS1-3 Analyze data from tests of two objects designed to solve the same problem to compare the strengths and weaknesses of how each performs.

Go online to access your digital course.

▶ VIDEO

📖 eTEXT

👆 INTERACTIVITY

▶ SCIENCE SONG

🎮 GAME

☑ ASSESSMENT

The Essential Question

How do the parts of plants and animals help them?

Show What You Know

Put an **X** on the part of the tortoise that protects it from other animals.

Quest Kickoff

STEM NATURE Copycats

How can you copy plant and animal parts to solve a problem?

Phenomenon Hi! I am Dr. Basha! I am a bioengineer. I make things that help people. I copy plant and animal parts.

Look for ways plants and animals use their parts to live. Use an animal or plant part to help solve a human problem. The path shows the Quest activities you will complete as you work through the topic. Check off your progress each time you complete an activity with a QUEST CHECK ✓ OFF.

1-LS1-1 Use materials to design a solution to a human problem by mimicking how plants and/or animals use their external parts to help them survive, grow, and meet their needs.

K-2-ETS1-2 Develop a simple sketch, drawing, or physical model to illustrate how the shape of an object helps it function as needed to solve a given problem.

Quest Check-In 2

Lesson 2 ●

Use what you learned about animal parts. Show how people copy an animal part.

Quest Check-In 3

Lesson 3 ◆

Show how plants and animals use their parts to meet their needs.

Quest Check-In 1

Lesson 1 ■

Use what you learned about plant parts. Show how people copy a plant part.

Quest Check-In Lab 4

Lesson 4 ▲

Find out how the color of a snowshoe hare's fur helps it stay alive.

Quest Findings

Complete the Quest! Copy a plant or animal part. Help solve a human problem.

How can you make a model of a plant?

Scientists use different materials to make models. The models help them study living things. What materials can you use to make a model of a plant?

Design and Build

☐ **1.** Look at the pictures of plants. Choose a plant.

☐ **2.** Choose your materials.

☐ **3.** Design and build your model.

Evaluate Your Model

4. Compare your model to the plant picture. Tell if your model shows all the parts of the plant.

5. Compare your model to models made by other students. Tell how the models are the same and different.

Materials

- pictures of plants

Suggested Materials

- poster board
- construction paper
- crayons
- small objects

Engineering Practice

You **make a model** to help you study the natural world.

Compare and Contrast

GAME

Practice what you learn with the Mini Games.

You can compare and contrast things. To compare means to see how things are the same. To contrast means to see how things are different.

Geese and Bike Riders

Geese fly in a V shape. The lead goose flies at the tip of the V. That goose flaps its wings. It makes streams of air that rise. The streams help the other geese save energy. A group of bike riders rides single file. The riders who follow the leader save energy.

☑ **Reading Check** Compare and Contrast
Underline how geese and bike riders are the same. Circle how they are different.

geese

bike riders

Plant Parts

▶ VIDEO

Watch a video about roots.

Vocabulary

root

stem

leaf

I can identify the major parts of plants.

I can explain how plant parts help plants.

1-LS1-1, K-2-ETS1-2

Jumpstart Discovery!

Look at the tree's leaves. Talk about how the leaves help the tree live. Look at the tree's trunk. Talk about how the trunk helps the tree live.

What do the *parts* of a plant look like?

Scientists study plant parts to learn what they do. How can you observe plant parts?

Materials
- a plant
- hand lens
- crayons

Procedure

☐ **1. Observe** the parts of the plant. Use all of the materials. Draw a picture of each part.

Science Practice

You **observe** to obtain and communicate information.

⚠ Wash your hands when done.

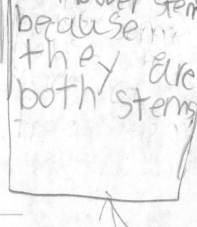

Analyze and Interpret Data

2. Explain how you think the shape of the stem helps the plant.

the stem helps because it's tall bats helps reach the sunlight.

3. Tell about an object that people make that is like a plant stem.

Roots

Plants have parts that help them get what they need to live and grow. Many plants have roots. A **root** is the part of a plant that takes in water.

Roots respond to gravity and moisture and grow into the soil. Roots hold the plant in the ground. Roots grow toward water. Roots get water and nutrients from the soil.

Identify Circle where water will go into the daffodil plants.

Quest Connection

Tell what features of roots people might want to copy. Why would people want to do this?

INTERACTIVITY

Go online to learn more about plant parts.

Stems and Leaves

Many plants have stems and leaves. Leaves and stems respond to the sun by growing toward it.

A **stem** is the part of a plant that takes water from the roots to the leaves and holds the plant up. Water and nutrients move from the roots. They move up the stem and into the leaves.

A **leaf** is the part of a plant that makes food. The leaves use sunlight, water, and nutrients to do this. The spines on a cactus are leaves. They protect the plant.

☑ **Reading Check** **Compare and Contrast** Draw a line under something a stem does. Draw a circle around something a leaf does.

roots

Flowers and Fruits

Many plants have flowers and fruits. Flowers and fruits help make new plants. Flowers contain eggs and pollen. These are used to make seeds. The fruit holds the seeds of a plant. The fruit keeps the seeds safe. Animals eat fruit. This helps seeds move from place to place.

Literacy ▸ Toolbox

Compare and Contrast Circle words that tell what flowers contain. Underline something fruit does.

Predict What are some ways seeds can move from one place to another?

_____

_____

_____

flowers and fruits

desert wildflowers

Quest Check-In

Roots Help Plants Survive

Some plants have just one thick root structure called a taproot. It goes deep into the soil and takes in water for the plant. The structure of the taproot helps the plant stay where it is.

Identify Find something in the picture that works like a taproot.

dandelion with taproot

tent stake

Animal Parts

▶ VIDEO

Go online to learn how animals use their senses.

Vocabulary

gills

scales

I can identify the major parts of animals.

I can explain how animal parts help animals.

1-LS1-1, K-2-ETS1-2, K-2- ETS1-3

Jumpstart Discovery!

Look at the leopard's eyes. Talk about how seeing helps it. Look at the leopard's paws. Talk about how paws help it move.

HANDS-ON LAB

1-LS1-1, K-2-ETS1-2, K-2-ETS1-3,
SEP.2, SEP.3, SEP.8

How do whiskers help a cat?

Scientists know that animals use their senses. Their senses tell about the environment. How do whiskers help a cat know how big an opening is?

Materials

- boxes or tubes with different-sized openings
- styrofoam ball
- tape
- pipe cleaners

Design and Build

☐ 1. Use the materials. Make a model of the head and whiskers of a cat.

☐ 2. Make a plan. Test how whiskers help a cat get through openings.

☐ 3. Test your model. Record your data.

Engineering Practice

You **use models** to see how structure is related to function.

Evaluate Your Design

4. Compare your observations with the observations from another group. Tell how the shape of the whiskers helps them give information to the cat.

How Animals Move

Animals have different body parts. Some body parts help animals move. Animals move to find food and water.

Many animals, like bears, have legs. Fish have fins. Horses and other animals have hooves. Birds have wings.

INTERACTIVITY

Go online to learn more about animal parts.

black bear

Explain Underline words that tell what animals use to move.

Crosscutting Concepts ▸ Toolbox

Structure and Function The shape of an animal's body parts give clues to how the animal moves. Look at the feet on the black bear. How do the feet help the bear move? Describe one way a bear might use its claws.

Body Coverings and Ways of Breathing

Animals' body coverings protect them. Hair or fur grows from the skin of many animals. Feathers grow from the skin of birds. Fish and snakes have hard plates called **scales**. Many ocean animals and insects have hard shells.

People and many animals have lungs. They draw in air through their noses. **Gills** are parts on fish that let them breathe underwater.

Identify Underline words that tell the names of different body coverings.

feathers on a bird

scales on a snake

gills on a fish

meerkat

Animals' Senses and Responses

Animals use their eyes to see. They use their ears to hear. A meerkat uses its ears to listen for danger. Animals smell things and taste things. They touch things with their bodies.

Animals' senses give them information about the world. The information helps them grow and live. Some information tells them they are in danger. Animals use their senses to stay safe.

Quest Connection

Animal eyes often see farther than human eyes. Tell a partner a tool people made to see farther.

Different Shapes, Different Uses

Different birds have different beaks.
Some beaks have sharp points.
Some beaks are shaped like hooks.

woodpecker

Differentiate Which beak is the right shape for making holes in trees? Circle it.

eagle

Analyze People make tools based on animal parts. Tell something people do with a pointed tool.

K-2-ETS1-1

▶ **VIDEO**

Watch a video about how bioengineers solve problems.

Design a Tool

Phenomenon Bioengineers study plant and animal parts. They might study a turtle shell to design a better bicycle helmet.

Would you like to help a bioengineer solve a problem?

tortoise

Design It

Animals use tools. Look at the photos. Design a tool you can use to solve a problem.

chimpanzee

☐ Choose an animal tool you will copy. Think about the tool you will make. What do you think people could use this tool for?

crow

_____

_____

_____

_____

_____

☐ Think of what you need to build the tool.

☐ Design the tool.

☐ Describe how your tool will work. How can you make it better?

_____

_____

_____

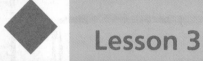

People Learn from Plant and Animal Parts

▶ **VIDEO**

Watch a video about biomimicry.

Vocabulary

mimic

I can demonstrate how people can learn from plant and animal parts.

_____

1-LS1-1

Jumpstart Discovery!

Be a leaf. Act it out. Tell how a leaf helps a plant live. Be a squirrel. Act it out. Tell how a squirrel's legs help it live.

What can people learn from an acorn shell?

Acorns fall from oak trees. How does the hard shell help the acorn?

Materials
- acorn
- hand lens
- small hammer

Procedure

☐ 1. Use all the materials. Make a plan to break the shell of the acorn. Show your plan to your teacher.

☐ 2. Conduct your investigation. Record your observations.

Science Practice

You **construct explanations** to explain phenomena.

⚠ Wear goggles if you are using a hammer.

Analyze and Interpret Data

3. **Explain** how the hard shell helps the acorn.

_____

_____

_____

4. How can people copy what the acorn does to help people stay alive?

_____

_____

People Mimic Nature

Plants and animals have different body parts. People look at how plants function. They look at how animals solve problems. People get ideas from other living things. People **mimic**, or copy, what plants and animals do. They do this to get what they need to live.

Quest Connection

Tell why people can get good ideas about solving problems from plants and animals.

barbed wire fence

Porcupines have sharp quills. Animals come near them. They raise their quills. Their quills keep animals from eating them. People mimicked how nature uses sharp things. People made fences with many sharp metal points. Farmers put their cows and sheep inside the fences. The fences keep animals from walking away.

INTERACTIVITY

Go online to learn about biomimicry.

porcupine

Predict Do you think people will ever stop getting ideas from other living things? Tell why or why not.

☑ **Reading Check** **Compare and Contrast** Underline words that show how porcupines use their quills to protect themselves.

burr

A Sticky Invention

Burrs are plant seeds that stick to things.

An inventor studied how burrs stick. He invented a fastener. One side has hooks like burrs. The other side has loops like fabric. The two sides stick together. People use hook-and-loop fasteners in products that help people. One product is a splint. It wraps around an arm, leg, hand, or foot. It holds broken bones or pulled muscles in place.

splint

Identify What is another way that people use hook-and-loop fasteners?

Order Objects by Length

Many kinds of plants have the same parts.
The parts are different sizes. Trees have
trunks. The trunks are different lengths.

Compare Look at the pictures.
Order the trunks by their lengths.
Label the longest trunk with a 1.
Label the shortest trunk with a 3.

Lesson 4

Where Plants and Animals Live

Vocabulary

environment

I can use my senses to observe living things in their environments.

1-LS1-1, K-2-ETS1-2

Jumpstart Discovery!

Draw a picture of a plant or animal. Talk about what the plant or animal needs to live. Talk about how it gets what it needs from where it lives.

uInvestigate Lab

What happens to a
water plant
out of water?

If you take a plant from where it lives, can it survive? Could a wetland plant live in a desert?

Materials

- wax paper
- string
- paper clips
- container with water
- scissors

Procedure

☐ **1.** Use the materials to build a model of a plant that lives in water.

☐ **2.** Make a plan to investigate what would happen if the water plant was on land.

☐ **3.** Record your observations.

Science Practice

You **build models** to study real-life phenomena.

 Be careful using scissors.

Analyze and Interpret Data

4. Evaluate What happened to your model water plant when it was on land? Tell a partner why.

5. Draw Conclusions Can the water plant live on land? Tell a partner.

Environments

Plants and animals live in environments. This is a lake environment. An **environment** is everything that is around a living thing. Nonliving things like water and air are part of environments. Living things like plants and animals are part of environments. People are part of environments, too. Living things get what they need in their environment.

Science Practice
▸Toolbox

Ask Questions Ask questions about environments to learn what kinds of plants and animals live in them.

Explain Underline nonliving things that are part of environments. Circle living things that are part of environments.

lake environment

Sensing Environments

You can use your senses to learn about environments. You can use your senses to learn about this forest environment. You can see things in an environment. You can hear things in an environment. You can touch things in an environment. You can smell things in an environment. You can use your senses to learn about this forest environment.

forest environment

Identify Circle words that tell how you use your senses.

Quest Connection

Tell how people use their senses to learn about environments. Tell how this helps them mimic nature.

Land and Water Environments

There are land and water environments. Living things get what they need in them. You can use your senses to learn about them.

☑ **Reading Check** **Compare and Contrast** Tell how a wetland is like an ocean. Tell how a wetland is different from an ocean.

Visual Literacy Look at the picture of a meadow. Write how the mouse is getting what it needs to live.

_____

- - - - - - - - - - - - - - - - - -

_____

- - - - - - - - - - - - - - - - - -

_____

- - - - - - - - - - - - - - - - - -

_____

The ocean is salt water. The water is very deep. Fish live there. Seaweed lives there.

It is very dry in a desert. The ground is sand or hard soil. Few plants and animals live there.

Many grasses live in a meadow. There are few trees. Birds and other small animals live there.

INTERACTIVITY

Go online to explore different environments.

Water covers the soil in a wetland. The water is not very deep. Birds and grasses live there.

Lesson 4 Where Plants and Animals Live 173

How do snowshoe hares stay safe?

Materials
- Landscape and Hares sheet
- crayons

People and animals use color to stay safe. Snowshoe hares have fur that is brown in the summer and white in the winter. Can you think of ways people use color when they are outside?

Science Practice

You **use a model** to answer questions about nature.

Procedure

☐ **1.** Look at the pictures of the snowshoe hares.

☐ **2.** Use the Landscape and Hares sheet to learn how the fur color of the hares keeps them safe.

☐ **3.** Record your notes in the chart.

Picture	How Color Affects the Animal or Environment
summer	
winter	
hares	

Analyze and Interpret Data

4. **Predict** What color is the fur on the hare likely to be in winter?

_____

_____

5. **Draw Conclusions** What might people learn from how animals use color? Tell a partner.

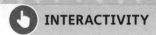
NATURE Copycats

How can you copy plant and animal parts to solve a problem?

Phenomenon Think about what you have learned about plant and animal parts. What can people learn from plants and animals?

Show What You Found

Now it is time for you to design a solution. It should be based on a plant or animal part. Draw a picture of your solution. Tell how your solution will help people.

QUEST CHECK ✓ OFF

Bioengineer

Bioengineers study plants and animals. They use what they learn to build things. Bioengineers make things that help sick or hurt people. They make artificial arms and legs. They try to solve other problems, too.

Some bioengineers work at colleges. Some work in hospitals. Some work for companies.

What problem would you try to solve if you were a bioengineer?

_____

_____

_____

_____

The Essential Question

How do the parts of plants and animals help them?

Show What You Learned

Tell a partner what you learned about how the parts of plants and animals help them live.

1. Look at the picture of the plant. Label the plant's parts. Use the word bank.

| roots   stem   leaves   flowers   fruit |

2. All species of cats see well at night. Which human technology is most likely to mimic the eyes of a cat?

    a. night vision glasses

    b. microscope

    c. telescope

    d. flashlight

3. Look at your answer to question 2. Write how people could use what they learned from a cat. Write what they could make to solve a human problem.

4. Explain how color can keep an animal safe.

Read this scenario and answer questions 1–4.

Engineers wanted to make a very fast train. They wanted the train to be quiet, too. That was a problem. Fast trains make a loud noise when they come out of tunnels. The engineers had to find a way to make a fast and quiet train.

The engineers looked at the kingfisher. This bird has a pointed beak. The kingfisher dives into the water to catch fish. It does not make the water splash. The engineers made the front of the train like the kingfisher's beak. The train is fast and quiet.

1. Which part of the kingfisher helps it dive into the water with no splash?

a. wings   **c.** feathers

b. beak   **d.** legs

2. Write how the engineers copied the kingfisher.

_____

- -

_____

- -

_____

3. Why can animals like the kingfisher do things that people cannot do?

   a. They have different body parts.

   b. They have different environments.

   c. They do not need things that people need.

   d. They need things that people do not need.

4. Circle the words that correctly complete the sentence.

desert   land   meadow   water

The kingfisher lives in a - - - - - - - - - - - environment.

How do the spines of cacti help them?

Phenomenon Cactus plants have spines. Spines are very sharp leaves. How can you use a model to test how spines help cacti?

Design and Build

☐ **1.** Study the picture of the cactus spines.

☐ **2.** Choose your materials to make a model.

☐ **3.** Design and build your model.

☐ **4.** Try to touch the stem without touching the spines. Try three times. Write what happens in the table.

Materials
- scissors
- crayons
- tape
- glue

Suggested Materials
- different types of paper
- variety of cardboard objects
- variety of long, thin objects

Engineering Practice

You **make a model** to help you study phenomena in nature.

Be careful using scissors and other objects with sharp points.

Observations

Trial Number	Observations
1	
2	
3	

Evaluate Your Model

5. **Identify** Show a partner the spines and stem on your model.

6. **Explain** Tell what would happen to an animal that tried to eat the cactus.

7. **Use Evidence** Tell how the spines help the cactus.

Parents and Offspring

Next Generation Science Standards

1-LS1-2: Read texts and use media to determine patterns in behavior of parents and offspring that help offspring survive.

1-LS3-1: Make observations to construct an evidence-based account that young plants and animals are like, but not exactly like, their parents.

Go online to access
your digital course.

▶ VIDEO

📖 eTEXT

👆 INTERACTIVITY

▶ SCIENCE SONG

🎮 GAME

☑ ASSESSMENT

The Essential Question

How are parents and their young alike and different?

Show What You Know

Circle the parent. Put an X on the young.

Find the Parents

What clues help us find a young animal's parent?

Phenomenon Hi! I'm Ms. Swift! I'm a nature scientist. I help keep plants and animals safe. I need your help.

Someone left a gate open at the zoo! Many animals escaped. Help me find the missing parents of these three young animals. Look for clues as you read. The path shows the Quest activities you will complete as you work through the topic. Check off your progress each time you complete an activity with a QUEST CHECK ✓ OFF .

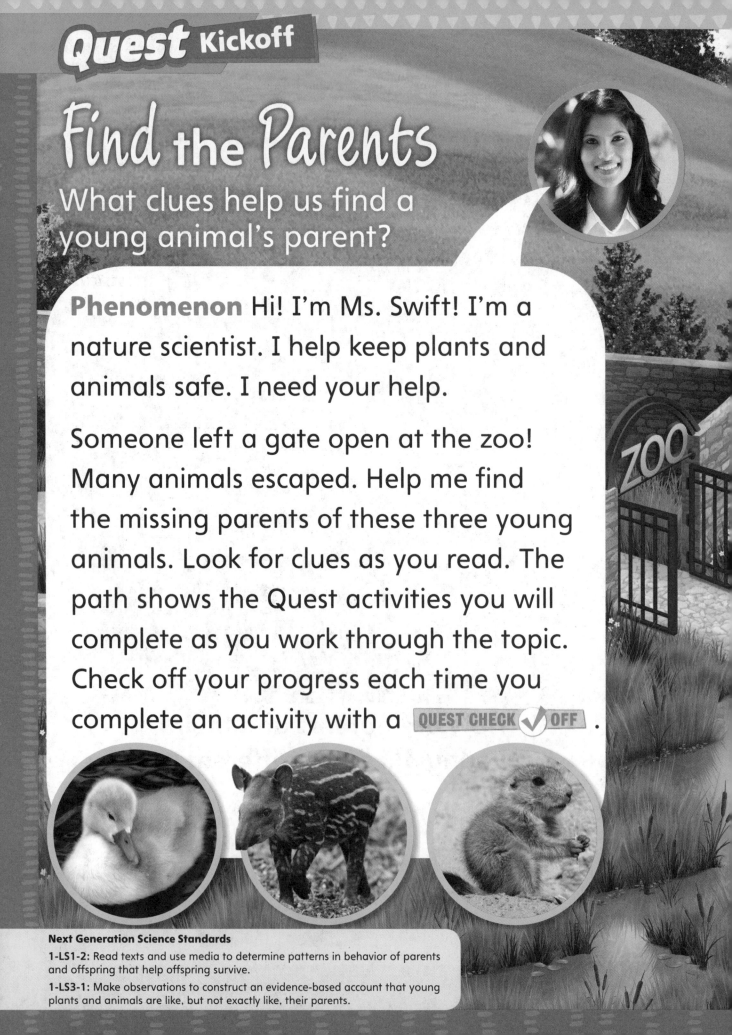

Next Generation Science Standards

1-LS1-2: Read texts and use media to determine patterns in behavior of parents and offspring that help offspring survive.

1-LS3-1: Make observations to construct an evidence-based account that young plants and animals are like, but not exactly like, their parents.

VIDEO

Watch a video about a nature scientist.

Quest Check-In 2

Lesson 2 ●

Use what you learned about parents and young to match the puppies to their parents.

Quest Check-In 3

Lesson 3 ◆

Read more about animal behaviors and how bear parents help their cubs.

Quest Check-In Lab 1

Lesson 1 ■

Use what you learned about animal life cycles to tell how two animal life cycles are alike and different.

Quest Findings

Complete the Quest! Find a fun way to show how the young animals and their parents are alike and different.

Which mouse is **longer?**

Nature scientists make observations of living things to answer questions. What observation can you make to answer the question in the title?

Science Practice

You **make observations** to help answer scientific questions.

Procedure

☐ **1.** Think of a way you can make observations to find out which mouse is longer.

☐ **2.** Collect and record your data.

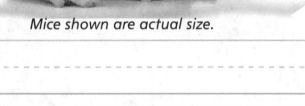

Mice shown are actual size.

Analyze and Interpret Data

3. Look at your data. Circle data that show which mouse is longer.

4. Tell how the mice are different.

Main Idea and Details

Nature scientists observe animals. Read about the main idea and details of geese and their young.

The main idea is what the sentences are about. Details tell about the main idea.

Geese and Their Young

Geese keep their young safe. They build nests for the young. The young sleep near their parents. Geese and their young find grass to eat. Parents stay near while young eat.

☑ **Reading Check** **Main Idea and Details**
Circle the main idea. Underline two details.

geese and their goslings

Plant and Animal Life Cycles

▶ **VIDEO**

Watch a video about life cycles.

Vocabulary

life cycle

offspring

I can observe the life cycles of some plants and animals.

1-LS1-2

Jumpstart Discovery!

Circle a tomato, red pepper, and cucumber in the picture. What do you think is inside each of these?

How do plants grow and change?

Nature scientists ask questions about plants. How do you know a plant grows and changes?

Procedure

☐ **1.** Choose one kind of seed.

☐ **2.** Use all of the other materials. Make a plan to see how seeds grow. Tell your teacher your plan before you start.

☐ **3. Observe** your seeds every other day for ten days. Draw what you observe.

Analyze and Interpret Data

4. Tell how the seeds changed.

Materials

- seeds (lima beans, radish, or sunflower)
- wet paper towel
- resealable plastic bag
- hand lens

Science Practice

You **make observations** to help answer a question.

Life Cycle of a Plant

A **life cycle** is the stages a living thing goes through during its life. A watermelon plant begins as a seed. Then it grows into a small plant. The plant changes. It grows into an adult plant.

Draw the missing arrow in the life cycle.

fruit with seeds

adult plant

young plant

Life Cycle of an Animal

Animals have life cycles, too. A tapir is an animal that lives in the forest. A young tapir will grow and change. It will look like its parents.

It will have **offspring**, or young, of its own.

☑ Reading Check

Main Idea and Details Circle the main idea. Underline two details.

newborn tapir

adult tapir

young tapir

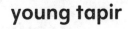

Quest Connection

Tell how the newborn tapir grows and changes.

How are the life cycles alike and different?

You have learned about the life cycle of a plant and an animal. Now find out how the life cycles of two animals are alike and different.

Materials
- Animal Life Cycles worksheet
- scissors
- glue stick

Procedure

☐ **1.** Choose two animals from the worksheet. Cut out each part of the two life cycles.

☐ **2.** Arrange the cycles in the two boxes. Paste them in each box.

☐ **3.** What can you add to each to make it a cycle? Add it.

☐ **4. Observe** how each animal grows and changes.

Science Practice

You **compare observations** to learn about patterns in nature.

⚠ **Be careful when using scissors.**

Analyze and Interpret Data

5. Describe the life cycle of each animal.

6. What patterns do you see?

Observe Parents and Young

Vocabulary

compare

contrast

I can understand that young plants and animals are like, but not exactly like, their parents.

1-LS3-1

Jumpstart Discovery!

Be a young plant. Act it out.
Be a parent plant. Act it out.
Talk about the two plants.

What do young plants look like?

Nature scientists can observe young plants. They make sure they are healthy like the parent plants.

Materials
- paper
- crayons

Science Practice

You **observe** when you look closely at things.

Procedure

☐ **1.** Look at the two parent plants.

☐ **2.** Choose one of the parent plants. Draw it on a piece of paper.

☐ **3.** What do you think the young plant of this parent would look like? Draw it.

Analyze and Interpret Data

4. Observe the young plants of the other groups. Tell what you notice.

Alike and Different

Young plants and animals look like their parents in some ways. They look different in other ways.

Compare these two animals. To **compare** is to tell how two things are alike. Contrast the two animals. To **contrast** is to tell how two things are different.

orangutans

Plants Are Alike

▶ VIDEO

Watch a video about parents and their young.

Plants of the same kind are alike. All marigold plants have colorful flowers.

A young plant and a parent plant are alike. They both have stems and leaves.

Look at these plants. The leaves on both plants look alike. They are the same shape.

Compare Circle the parts of the plants that are alike.

young marigold plant

parent marigold plant

Plants Are Different

Plants of the same kind are different. Hyacinth flowers can have different colors.

hyacinths

A young plant and a parent plant are different. The plants are different sizes.

Parent plants have more leaves. Parent plants often have more flowers.

☑ Reading Check **Main Idea and Details**
Underline a detail about parents.

Draw a young plant and its parent.

Animals Are Alike

Animals of the same kind are alike.
All prairie dogs have fur.

Young animals and their parents are alike.
Prairie dogs have the same body parts.
Their faces are the same shape.

INTERACTIVITY

Compare how living things and their parents are alike and different.

Compare Circle two ways parents and young are alike.

Quest Connection

Tell what clues will help you find the missing parents.

prairie dogs

Animals Are Different

Animals of the same kind are different. Rabbits can be brown, black, or white.

Young animals and their parents are different, too. Young rabbits are smaller than their parents.

Contrast Draw an **X** on a rabbit that is different from the others.

Math ▸ Toolbox

Compare Numbers
You can compare how long objects are. Parent rabbits have longer ears than young rabbits. Use cubes to measure the lengths of two classroom objects. Which is longer?

rabbits

Alike and Different

Puppies may look like their parents.
Puppies may look different, too.

Airedale

St. Bernard

Identify Match the puppies to their parents.

Contrast Tell how the puppies look different from one another.

uEngineer It! | Design | STEM

INTERACTIVITY

Go online to learn about code for computers.

Code the Way!

Phenomenon Game code turns the player's movements into actions in the game.

Would you like to write code for video games?

Learn about a career as a software engineer.

gamers

Design It

Video games use codes to make the characters move. Build a code for a video game. Help the robot owl reach the young owlets.

- ☐ Use a coin to represent a robot owl.

- ☐ Place the coin in the top left square.

- ☐ Use the **symbol key** to write code. Guide the robot owl through the maze.

Your Code

1.	2.	3.	4.	5.	6.
7.	8.	9.	10.	11.	12.

Patterns in Animal Behavior

Vocabulary

protect

pattern

behavior

I can tell what animals need.
I can explain how the behaviors of parents and their young help the young survive.

1-LS1-2

Jumpstart Discovery!

Think of an animal home.

Draw it on a sheet of paper.

How did it help the young animals?

Tell a partner what you know.

How do nests protect eggs?

Parent birds build nests. Nests protect the eggs.

Design and Build

☐ **1.** Circle the materials you will use to build your nest.

☐ **2.** Design your nest. Build it.

☐ **3.** Place marbles in your nest.

Evaluate Your Design

4. Tell how your nest helps protect the marbles.

5. How is your nest like a bird's nest?

Materials

- 1-inch marbles
- nest materials (paper, newspaper, leaves, small paper bags, grass, twigs, modeling clay)

Engineering Practice

You **plan a design** before you build something.

 Wash your hands when you are done.

Animal Needs

An animal needs food. An animal needs water. An animal needs shelter.

wood mouse

Identify Circle a photo that shows shelter.

Underline a photo that shows food.

red fox

bears

Parents Help Young

▶ VIDEO

Watch a video about animal behavior.

lions

woodpeckers

Parents feed their young.
They help young find water.

Identify Circle the parent in each photo.

Quest Connection

Tell why young animals need their parents.

Parents Protect Young

Many young animals have parents that protect them. To **protect** something is to keep it from danger. Parents may protect their young from the cold.

meerkats

swans

kangaroos

Crosscutting Concepts ▸ Toolbox

Patterns Scientists look for patterns when they observe nature. Nature has many patterns. A **pattern** is something that repeats. Parents protect their young. They use their bodies to protect them. What patterns do you see on these two pages? How do these pictures show evidence that parents protect their young?

penguins

cats

Lesson 3   Patterns in Animal Behavior   ⟨211⟩

Parents Teach Young

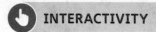

INTERACTIVITY

Show how parents take care of their young.

Parent elephants teach their young different ways to act, or **behavior**. They show how to use their trunks. They show how to roll in mud. Mud keeps their skin safe from the sun.

Identify Underline two things parent elephants teach.
Circle the young in the pictures.

elephants

Young Stay Close and Make Sounds

Young stay close to a parent to stay warm. Young stay close to a parent to sleep. Young hold on to a parent to stay safe.

Young also help their parents. They cry and chirp to show they are hungry.

☑ Reading Check Main Idea and Details Underline one detail about the young.

koalas

birds

whales

Parents Help Young Learn

The grizzly bear cares for her cubs.

She feeds them and protects them.

The cubs learn to hide when in danger.

The black bear cares for her cubs.

She feeds them and protects them.

The cubs learn to climb trees to stay safe.

☑ **Reading Check** Main Idea and Details

Underline ways mother bears help.

Circle what the cubs learn.

black bears

grizzly bears

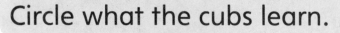

Compare Numbers

The symbol > means more than.

The symbol < means less than.

Some animals live in groups.
You can use symbols to compare
the number of animals in each group.

Count The animals in each group.
Write the numbers in the boxes.

fish

turtles

Compare Write the correct symbol
in the sentence.

The number of fish is [ ] the number of turtles.

⏺ **INTERACTIVITY**

Apply what you learned in the Quest.

Find the Parents

What clues help us find a young animal's parent?

Phenomenon Look back through the pages. Find the parent that matches each of these young.

Show What You Found

You have found the young animals and their parents. Choose one. Draw the parent and young animal or make models from clay. Then write how the parent helps their young.

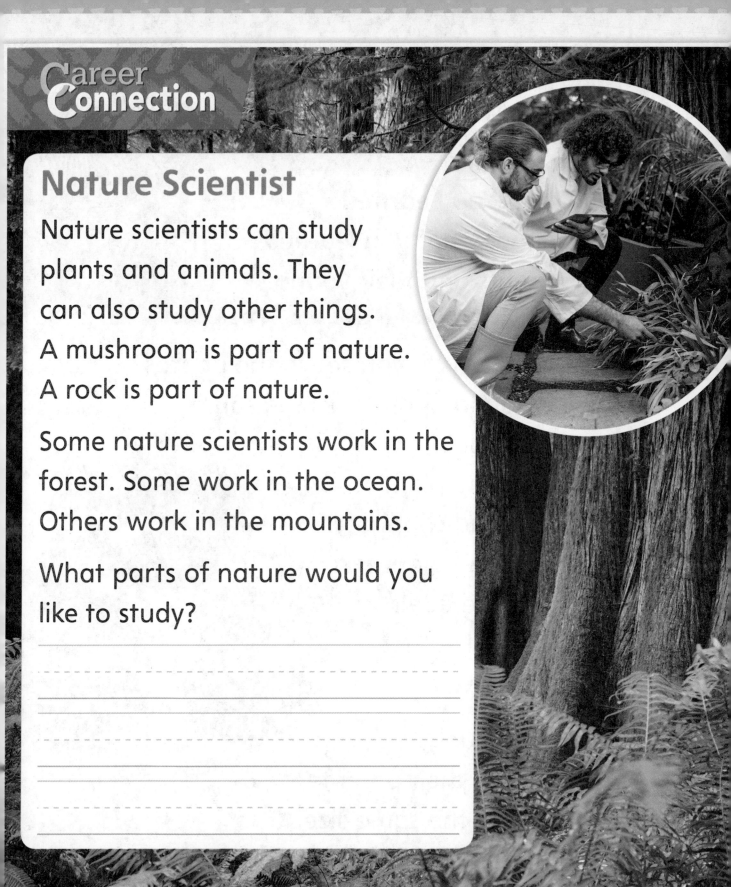

Career Connection

Nature Scientist

Nature scientists can study plants and animals. They can also study other things. A mushroom is part of nature. A rock is part of nature.

Some nature scientists work in the forest. Some work in the ocean. Others work in the mountains.

What parts of nature would you like to study?

_____

_____

_____

_____

_____

The Essential Question

How are parents and their young alike and different?

Show What You Learned

Tell a partner what you learned about parents and their young.

1. What pattern do you see in the photos?
   a. The young plant looks the same as the adult tree.
   b. The young plant grows and changes.
   c. The young plant is as tall as the adult.
   d. The seedling has more leaves.

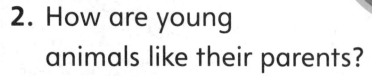

2. How are young animals like their parents?
   a. They are the same size.
   b. They are a different color.
   c. They have the same body parts.
   d. They have different behaviors.

3. How do young animals survive?
Use the word bank to fill in this table.

teach cry learn protect feed stay close

Things Parents Do	Things Young Do

4. Look at the photo of the young zebra
and its parent. Write how the young's
behavior helps it live.

_____

_____

_____

_____

_____

Read and answer questions 1–4.

Diego got a fish tank for his birthday. He put rocks and water plants in his tank. He bought orange guppies and red platies. The fish swim all over the tank.

One day, a fish had babies. The young were very small. They had to hide from the big fish. They stayed together among the plants. They were hard to find. They only came out when Diego put food in the tank.

1. Which statement best describes how the young fish are like their parents?
   a. The young fish are the same size as the parents.
   b. The young fish might get eaten by bigger fish.
   c. The young fish have the same shape as the parents.
   d. The young fish hid in the plants.

2. Write how the baby fish and the adults have different behaviors.

_____

- - - - - - - - - - - - - - - - - - - -

_____

- - - - - - - - - - - - - - - - - - - -

_____

- - - - - - - - - - - - - - - - - - - -

_____

3. Diego gave one of his young fish to a friend. What kind of fish could it be?

   a. a green platy

   b. an orange platy

   c. a red guppy

   d. an orange guppy

4. Circle the word that correctly completes the sentence.

| danger   water   food   shelter |

Diego put plants in his tank because young fish need _____.

How do living things change as they grow?

Materials
- fishing line
- plastic stirrer
- pipe cleaner
- craft stick

Phenomenon Each material models part of a living thing. You will use these materials to observe the difference between the young and the parent.

Procedure

Science Practice

You **observe** when you look closely at things.

☐ **1. Observe** the fishing line. This is like the quill of a young porcupine. Write what you observe in the table.

☐ **2. Observe** the stirrer. This is like the quill of a parent porcupine. Write what you observe in the table.

porcupines

☐ **3. Observe** the pipe cleaner. This is like the stem of a young plant. Write what you observe in the table.

⚠️ **Use care when handling pointed objects.**

☐ **4. Observe** the craft stick. This is like the stem of a parent plant. Write what you observe in the table.

Observations

Object	Observations
fishing line	
stirrer	
pipe cleaner	
craft stick	

Analyze and Interpret Data

5. **Explain** how a young porcupine is like and different from its parent.

6. **Explain** how a young plant is like and different from its parent.

Science Practices

Questions

Scientists ask questions about the world. They could ask which rocks float in water. This question can be tested. Scientists can do tests to find the answer. A scientist would not ask which rocks are pretty. This question cannot be tested because people like different rocks.

Ask one question that you have about these rocks. Tell if your question can be tested.

Investigations

Scientists look for answers. They investigate. They do fair tests. In a fair test, you change one thing. Then you see what happens. You could drop a rock to see if it breaks. Then you can try a different rock. But you must drop it from the same height. If you change the height, the test is not fair.

A scientist puts a big rock in fresh water. He puts a small rock in salt water. Tell if this is a fair test. Explain why or why not.

_____

_____

_____

_____

_____

Science Practices

Tools

Scientists observe things to learn about them. What they learn is called information. Scientists can use their senses to get information. They can look and listen. They can also use tools to get more information. They can use a balance to measure weight. They can use a graduated cylinder to measure liquids. They can use a metric ruler to measure length.

Circle the tool you could use to measure the length of the crystal.

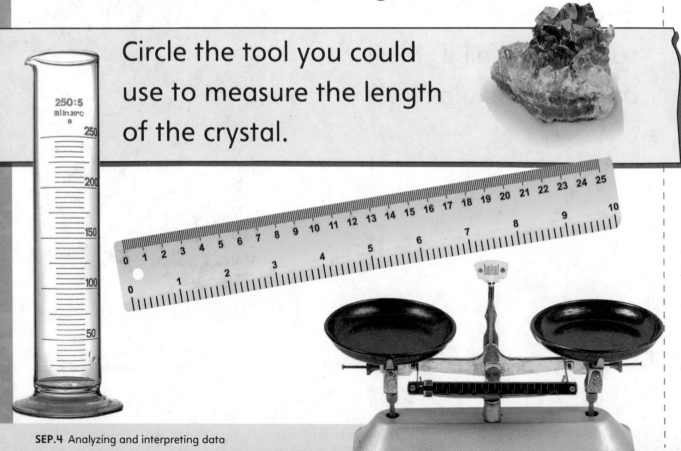

Information is important. Sometimes it is hard to remember all the information. Scientists do not want to forget what they have learned. They record all the information that they find. They draw or write what they observe. They use notebooks and computers.

What kind of information could you collect about these minerals? What tools can you use to observe?

Science Practices

Analyze and Interpret Data

What kinds of rocks are in rivers? A scientist would not just guess. She would collect information, or data. She would analyze and interpret the data. You interpret data when you try to understand what it means.

There are fossils in some rocks.

Observe the fossil. Draw what you think this place looked like when the animal was alive.

How to Measure

Scientists can measure very small or very large things. They must use the correct tools. You can measure a pencil with a metric ruler. A grain of sand would be hard to measure. Scientists measure things carefully. They may measure something more than once.

Which tool would you use to measure the fossil? Explain to a partner how to use that tool.

Science Practices

Explanations

You explain something when you help others understand it. Scientists can draw or build a model to explain how something works. A model is a copy of a real thing. When you draw something, you are making a model.

This drawing shows layers of soil.

Draw a model of something you like. Add labels to show how it works.

SEP.2 Developing and using models
SEP.6 Constructing explanations and designing solutions
SEP.7 Engaging in argument from evidence

Arguments from Evidence

Scientists share what they know. They use arguments and evidence. In an argument, you tell what you know. You also tell why you think it is true. The facts that show that something is true are called evidence. Scientists use data as evidence.

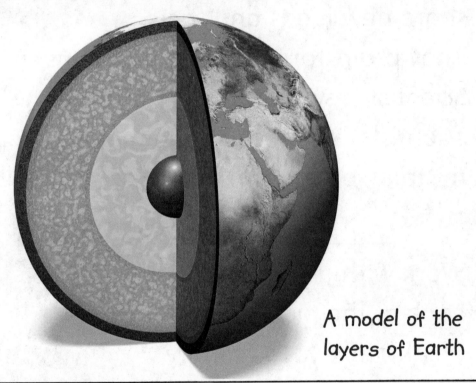

A model of the layers of Earth

Look at the model of Earth. How could a scientist find evidence that the layers inside Earth are hot?

_____

_____

_____

_____

Science Practices

Teamwork

Scientists often work together. They can get information from other scientists. They share new ideas and facts. They brainstorm to solve problems. Scientists review the work of other scientists. When someone makes a mistake, others can help.

Real gold has rounder edges and is shinier than fool's gold.

Work with a partner.
Look at the pictures.
Think of ways to identify
which mineral is gold
and which is not.

_____

_____

_____

_____

_____

Communication

Scientists communicate their work. Sometimes they present their work in person. Sometimes they write papers. Sometimes they write books. They share what they find with each other. They learn from the work of others. They describe what they observe. Scientists also share with the community.

Circle two ways that scientists share their findings.

Engineering Practices

Define a Problem

Engineers try to find answers to problems. Their work helps a community. They start by defining a problem they can solve.

Tell what problem the engineers were trying to solve when they designed the machines in the rock quarry.

machine

Design a Solution

Next, engineers design different ways to solve a problem. They test their solutions. Each test is a fair test. They can use models to help them.

This rock contains copper that can be used to make wires.

Copper is used to make wires and pipes in homes. Electricity can run through copper wires. Tell how engineers can test copper wires.

Engineering Practices

Improve the Design

Engineers are always looking for a better solution. They do tests. They collect and record data. They use data from other engineers. They analyze and interpret the data. Engineers use data as evidence. They use it to improve their solution.

Work with a partner.
Tell how you would improve the design of a tunnel through a mountain.

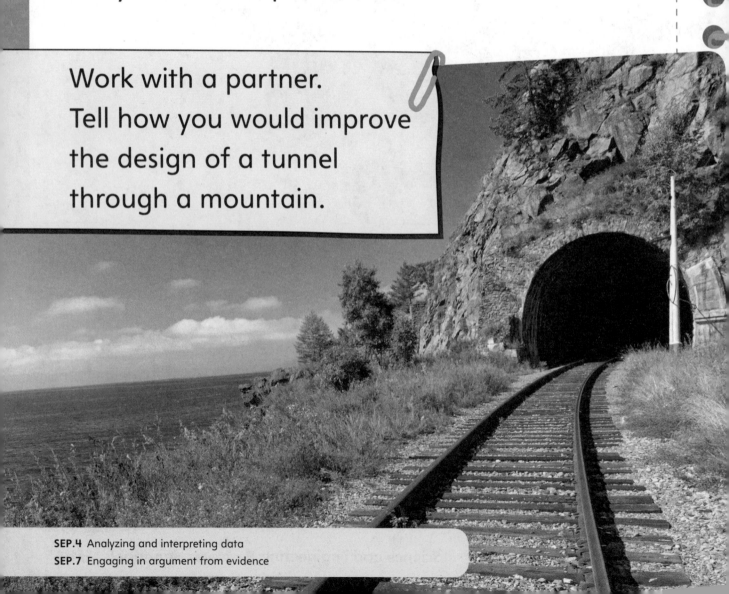

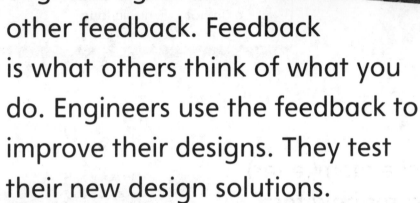

Engineers share their work with others. They review the work of others. Engineers give each other feedback. Feedback is what others think of what you do. Engineers use the feedback to improve their designs. They test their new design solutions.

What tools and information would you use to work on the tunnel problem?

_____

_____

_____

_____

Glossary

The glossary uses letters and signs to show how words are pronounced. The mark ' is placed after a syllable with a primary or heavy accent. The mark ' is placed after a syllable with a secondary or lighter accent.

anemometer (an' ə mom' ə tər) A tool that measures how fast wind moves. The **anemometer** showed the wind was moving very fast.

behavior (bi hā' vyər) A way of acting. Rolling in mud is a **behavior** of elephants.

blizzard (bliz' ərd) A storm with very high winds and snow. The **blizzard** knocked down a tree in my yard.

communicate (kə myü′ nə kāt)
To share a message or information.
I wrote a note to **communicate** with
my friend.

compare (kəm pâr′) To tell how two
things are alike. You can **compare** the
shapes of two oranges.

contrast (kən trast′) To tell how two
things are different. You can **contrast**
the shapes of a banana and an apple.

environment (en vī′ rən
mənt)) All of the living things
and nonliving things in a
place. A forest **environment**
has trees, water, and soil.

gill (gil) The part of a fish that helps it breathe underwater. The **gills** of a goldfish are near its head.

gravity (grav′ ə tē) A force that pulls objects toward Earth. **Gravity** causes rain to fall from clouds to the ground.

leaf (lēf) The part of a plant that makes food. **Leaves** of some trees change color in the fall.

life cycle (līf′ sī′ kəl) The stages a living thing goes through during its life. An apple tree grows flowers during its **life cycle.**

light (līt) What allows you to see people and things. The **light** from my lamp helps me see the picture.

living things (liv′ ing things) Things that need food and water, and that can grow and have young. A kitten is a **living thing.**

matter (mat′ ər) Anything that takes up space. A book is made of **matter.**

mimic (mim′ ik) To copy the way something looks or the way it acts. People **mimic** things that plants and animals do.

moon phase (mün′ fāz) The changing shapes of the moon in the sky. The full moon is a **moon phase.**

nonliving things (non liv′ ing things) Things that do not need food or water and that cannot grow or have young. A rock is a **nonliving thing.**

nutrient (nü′ trē ənt) Material in food that helps a body grow and stay healthy. Milk has many important **nutrients**.

offspring (òf′ spring′) The young produced by parents. A puppy is the **offspring** of a parent dog.

opaque (ō pāk′) Not letting light through. A wooden door is **opaque**.

pattern (pat′ ərn) Something that repeats. The changing shapes of the moon form a **pattern**.

percussion (pər kush′ ən) Musical instruments you strike to make sound. Drums are my favorite type of **percussion**.

pitch (pich) How high or low a sound is. The baby cried at a high **pitch.**

protect (prə tekt´) To keep something from danger. A mother bear **protects** her young cubs.

rain gauge (rān´ gāj) A tool that measures how much rain has fallen. The **rain gauge** showed there was more rain today than yesterday.

reflect (ri flekt´) To let light bounce off of. The lake water can **reflect** sunlight.

root (rüt) The part of a plant that grows into soil. A tree **root** may be very deep.

rotation (rō tā´ shən) The spinning of an object. The **rotation** of Earth causes day and night.

scale (skāl) One of many hard plates that cover the skin of snakes and fish. Some fish have very colorful **scales**.

season (sē′ zn) A time of the year that has a certain kind of weather and amount of sunlight. Summer is my favorite **season** of the year.

shadow (shad′ ō) A dark shape that is made when light is blocked. My cat made a **shadow** when she walked in front of the lamp.

shelter (shel′ tər) A place that provides protection. Caves provide **shelter** for many types of animals.

star (stär) A large ball of hot gas in space. A **star** looks small because it is very far away.

stem (stem) The part of a plant that holds it up. The **stem** of a rose has sharp thorns.

sun (sun) The closest star to Earth. The **sun** is what makes the day sky bright.

sunrise (sun′ rīz′) What happens when the sun seems to come up in the sky in the morning. Many people get up each day at **sunrise**.

sunset (sun′ set′) What happens when the sun seems to go down in the evening. Some animals like to hunt for food at **sunset**.

thermometer (thər mom′ ə tər) A tool that measures temperature. The **thermometer** shows me how hot or cold it is outside.

tornado (tôr nā′ dō) A storm with very high winds. A **tornado** is shaped like a funnel.

translucent (tran slü′ snt) Letting some light through but not all of it. The colored glass in the window is **translucent.**

transparent (tran spâr′ ənt) Letting almost all light through. My water glass is **transparent** because I can see through it.

vibrate (vī ′ brāt) To move back and forth very quickly. The drum top **vibrates** when I strike it.

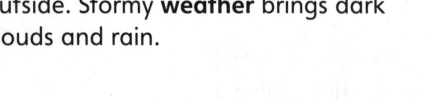

volume (vol′ yəm) How loud or soft a sound is. The **volume** of the radio is too loud.

weather (weth′ ər) How it feels and looks outside. Stormy **weather** brings dark clouds and rain.

Index

Index

Illustrations

Peter Bull Art Studio; Sara Lynn Cramb/Astound US; Peter Francis/MB Artists, Inc.; Lauren Gallegos/C.A. Tugeau, LLC; Patrick Gnan/IllustrationOnline.com; Bob Kayganich/IllustrationOnline.com; Kristen Kest/MB Artists, Inc.; Erika LeBarre/IllustrationOnline.com; Matt LeBarre/Blasco Creative, LLC; Lisa Manuzak/Astound; Precision Graphics/Lachina Publishing Services; Geoffrey P Smith; Jamie Smith/MB Artists, Inc.; Mark Rogalski/Painted Words, Inc.; Mike Rothman/Melissa Turk; Ralph Voltz/IllustrationOnline.com

Photographs

Photo locators denoted as follows: Top (T), Center (C), Bottom (B), Left (L), Right (R), Background (Bkgd)

Covers

Front Cover: Geoff Valcourt Images/Moment Open/Getty Images; Back Cover: Marinello/DigitalVision Vectors/Getty Images;

Front Matter

iv: Clari Massimiliano/Shutterstock; vi: Inmagineasia/Getty Images; vii: Monkey Business Images/Shutterstock; viii: Lucentius/iStock/Getty Images; ix: DmitriMaruta/iStock/Getty Images; x: Amble Design/Shutterstock; xi: Michaeljung/Shutterstock; xii Bkgrd: Brian J. Skerry/National Geographic/Getty Images; xii TR: Old Apple/Shutterstock; xiii B: Pearson Education; xiii TL: Pearson Education

Topic 1

000: Victor Korchenko/Alamy Stock Photo; 002: Inmagineasia/Getty Images; 004: Ekler/Shutterstock; 005: Maturos Thipmunee/EyeEm/Getty Images; 006: Blend Images KidStock/Brand X Pictures/Getty Images; 007: Exopixel/Shutterstock; 008: Carloscastilla/iStock/Getty Images; 009 B: S7chvetik/Shutterstock; 009 BC: Inmagineasia/Getty Images; 009 TR: Welcomia/Shutterstock; 010 B: Debbie DiCarlo Photography/Moment Open/Getty Images; 010 TL: Inmagineasia/Getty Images; 012: Ian Allenden/Alamy Stock Photo; 013: Sunny_baby/Shutterstock; 014: Sasra Adhiwana/EyeEm/Getty Images; 015 CL: Wavebreakmedia/Shutterstock; 015 CR: Tudor Photography/Pearson Education Ltd; 016 BR: Gannet77/iStock/Getty Images; 016 CR: MBI/Alamy Stock Photo; 016 TR: F1online digitale Bildagentur GmbH/Alamy Stock Photo; 017 BCR: Inmagineasia/Getty Images; 017 BR: Eleonora Cecchini/Moment/Getty Images; 017 TL: Glowimages RM/Alamy Stock Photo; 017 TR: Robertharding/Alamy Stock Photo; 018 B: Veniamin Kraskov/Shutterstock; 018 C: Inmagineasia/Getty Images; 020: David Woolley/DigitalVision/Getty Images; 021: JRLPhotographer/iStock/Getty Images Plus; 022 Bkgrd: Hung Chung Chih/Shutterstock; 022 BL: Juan Ignacio Sánchez Lara/Moment Open/Getty Images; 023 BCR: Theo Allofs/Corbis/Getty Images; 023 BR: Scyther5/Shutterstock; 023 TCR: Btkstudio/E+/Getty Images; 023 TR: Adrio Communications Ltd/Shutterstock; 024 B: Ariel Skelley/Blend Images/Getty Images; 024 CR: Inmagineasia/Getty Images; 026: Rvlsoft/Shutterstock; 027: James BO Insogna/Shutterstock; 028 Bkgrd: OJO Images Ltd/Alamy Stock Photo; 028 C: Inmagineasia/Getty Images; 029 B: Ted Foxx/Alamy Stock Photo;

029 TR: LWA/DigitalVision/Getty Imges; 030: Eleonora Cecchini/Moment/Getty Images; 031 BC: David Woolley/DigitalVision/Getty Images; 031 BCL: Btkstudio/E+/Getty Images; 031 BCR: Natthawut Nungsanther/EyeEm/Getty Images; 031 BL: Ian Allenden/Alamy Stock Photo; 031 BR: Adrio Communications Ltd/Shutterstock; 031 C: Scyther5/Shutterstock; 034: KidStock/Blend Images/Getty Images

Topic 2

036: Fraser Hall/Publisher Mix/Getty Images; 038: Monkey Business Images/Shutterstock; 041: Eliks/Shutterstock; 042: Maskot/Getty Images; 044: Shaiith/iStock/Getty Images; 045: Monkey Business Images/Shutterstock; 046: Frans Lemmens/Corbis Unreleased/Getty Images; 047 BR: Pakhnyushchy/Shutterstock; 047 CR: Lamai Prasitsuwan/123RF; 047 TL: Monkey Business Images/Shutterstock; 047 TR: Miguel Guerra/EyeEm/Getty Images; 048: Chris Howey/Shutterstock; 052 B: Look Aod27/Shutterstock; 052 TR: Afrijal Dahrin/EyeEm/Getty Images; 053 BR: Monkey Business Images/Shutterstock; 053 CR: Manzrussali/Shutterstock; 054 B: Richard Megna/Fundamental Photographs; 054 BL: Jacqui Dracup/Alamy Stock Photo; 054 TL: Monkey Business Images/Shutterstock; 055 B: Karramba Production/Shutterstock; 055 CR: Shutterstock; 056 Bkgrd: Iakov Kalinin; 056 C: Avtk/Shutterstock; 059: Dinozzaver/Shutterstock; 060: Anna Om/Shutterstock; 061 B: Cleanfotos/Shutterstock; 061 TR: Pidjoe/E+/Getty Images; 062 BCL: Allanw/Shutterstock; 062 BL: Andrey Bayda/Shutterstock; 062 BR: Bowdenimages/iStock/Getty Images; 062 TR: Salajean/Shutterstock; 063 BCR: Monkey Business Images/Shutterstock; 063 BL: Aurora Photos/Alamy Stock Photo; 063 BR: Solareven/Shutterstock; 063 CR: Wayne Matthew Syvinski/Shutterstock; 063 TR: Robandrew/E+/Getty Images; 064: Monkey Business Images/Shutterstock; 065: Olena Zaskochenko/Shutterstock; 066 Bkgrd: Shotshop GmbH/Alamy Stock Photo; 066 TR: Monkey Business Images/Shutterstock; 067 Bkgrd: Wildjohny/Shutterstock; 067 TR: Wavebreakmedia/Shutterstock; 068 BR: Erik Isakson/Blend Images/Getty Images; 068 T: Kryssia Campos/Moment Open/Getty Images; 069 C: Nexus 7/Shutterstock; 069 CL: Bancha SaeLao/Shutterstock; 069 CR: Thanatham Piriyakarnjanakul/EyeEm/Getty Images; 072: Michael Wheatley/Alamy Stock Photo

Topic 3

074: John Davis/Stocktrek Images/Getty Images; 076: Lucentius/iStock/Getty Images; 079 Bkgrd: B.A.E. Inc./Alamy Stock Photo; 079 CR: Dennis Hallinan/Alamy Stock Photo; 080: Nata777_7/Fotolia; 081: Artur Marfin/Shutterstock; 082 B: Katrin Lillenthal/EyeEm/Getty Images; 082 Bkgrd: AlinaMD/iStock/Getty Images; 083: Lucentius/iStock/Getty Images; 084 Bkgrd: Spiderstock/iStock/Getty Images; 084 TR: Godrick/Shutterstock; 085: Lucentius/iStock/Getty Images; 086: Terry Why/Photolibrary/Getty Images; 088: AlinaMD/Shutterstock; 089 B: Westend61/Brand X Pictures/Getty Images; 089 TR: Sergii Broshevan/123RF; 090: PavleMarjanovic/Shutterstock; 091 Bkgrd: Aliaksei Lasevich/Fotolia; 091 BR: Lucentius/iStock/Getty Images; 091 TR: Astrobobo/iStock/Getty Images Plus; 092 C: Luxx Images/DigitalVision/Getty Images; 092 TL: Lucentius/iStock/Getty Images; 092 TR: Paola Cravino Photography/Moment/Getty Images; 093: Pandawild/Fotolia; 094: Aleksandr Belugin/Alamy Stock Photo; 096 BR: FotoMak/Fotolia; 096 C: Lucentius/iStock/Getty Images; 096

TR: Creative Travel Projects/Shutterstock; 097: Snehit/Shutterstock; 098 BR: Tatiana Popova/123RF; 098 TR: Lucentius/iStock/Getty Images; 099 B: Bunya541/Moment Open/Getty Images; 099 TR: Tatiana Popova/123RF; 102 Bkgrd: Standret/iStock/Getty Images Plus; 102 CL: AlinaMD/iStock/Getty Images; 102 CR: Lucentius/iStock/Getty Images; 103 BR: Erik Isakson/Getty Images; 103 TR: NASA Photo/Alamy Stock Photo; 104 BR: Claudio Divizia/Fotolia; 104 T: Pockygallery/Shutterstock; 108: Gay Bumgarner/Alamy Stock Photo

Topic 4

110: Maxblack/Moment/Getty Images; 112: DmitriMaruta/iStock/Getty Images; 115: Rudy Lopez Photograph/Shutterstock; 118: Mandritoiu/Shutterstock; 119 BR: DmitriMaruta/iStock/Getty Images; 119 CR: TerryM/Shutterstock; 120 CR: Manfredxy/Shutterstock; 120 TR: Eakkachai Halang/Shutterstock; 121 Bkgrd: Minerva Studio/Shutterstock; 121 BL: Gary Hebding Jr./Alamy Stock Photo; 122 Bkgrd: Adam1975/123RF; 122 R: TerryM/Shutterstock; 122 TL: DmitriMaruta/iStock/Getty Images; 123 B: Evgeny Murtola/Shutterstock; 123 TR: NASA/NOAA GOES Project; 124: AdShooter/iStock/Getty Images; 126: JERRY_WANG/Shutterstock; 128 BC: DmitriMaruta/iStock/Getty Images; 128 BR: Stanley45/iStock/Getty Images; 128 TR: LiliGraphie/Shutterstock; 129 B: Mustafahacalaki/DigitalVision Vectors/Getty Images; 129 BL: ElenaBelozorova/iStock/Getty Images; 129 BR: Konradlew/Vetta/Getty Images; 130 BL: Werner Van Steen/DigitalVision/Getty Images; 130 BR: Sjo/iStock/Getty Images; 131 BL: Vovan/Shutterstock; 131 BR: AVTG/iStock/Getty Images; 132: DmitriMaruta/iStock/Getty Images; 134 Bkgrd: Blend Images/Alamy Stock Photo; 134 BR: DmitriMaruta/iStock/Getty Images; 135 Bkgrd: Ryan McGinnis/Moment/Getty Images; 135 TR: Mark Ferguson/Alamy Stock Photo; 136 BR: Andrew Kearton/Alamy Stock Photo; 136 T: Sjo/iStock/Getty Images; 137 BL: Vladitto/Shutterstock; 137 BR: Odon Arianna/Shutterstock; 138: Hepatus/Vetta/Getty Images

Topic 5

142: Blickwinkel/Alamy Stock Photo; 144: Amble Design/Shutterstock; 146: Filipe B. Varela/Shutterstock; 147 Bkgrd: Dan Sullivan/Alamy Stock Photo; 147 TR: Gino Santa Maria/Fotolia; 150 Bkgrd: William Turner/DigitalVision/Getty Images; 150 CR: Amble Design/Shutterstock; 152 BL: Igor Plotnikov/Shutterstock; 152 BR: Marketa Mark/Shutterstock; 153 B: Hero Images/DigitalVision/Getty Images; 153 TL: Amble Design/Shutterstock; 153 TR: Richard Griffin/123RF; 154: Matt/Fotolia; 155: Suponev Vladimir/Shutterstock; 156 Bkgrd: Isabelle Bonaire/Fotolia; 156 TR: Christian Colista/Shutterstock; 157 CR: Mgkuijpers/123RF; 157 TR: Hummingbird Art/Fotolia; 158 BC: Amble Design/Shutterstock; 158 R: Admir Basic/Fotolia; 159 B: Steve Mann/Shutterstock; 159 TL: Amble Design/Shutterstock; 159 TR: Deb Campbell/Shutterstock; 160 B: ImageBROKER/Alamy Stock Photo; 160 TR: Blickwinkel/Alamy Stock Photo; 161: Thierry Van Baelinghem/Science Source; 164 Bkgrd: Chris Winsor/Moment/Getty Images; 164 C: Amble Design/Shutterstock; 165: Greatstock/Alamy Stock Photo; 166 BR: Ktaylorg/iStock/Getty Images; 166 TL: Amble Design/Shutterstock; 166 TR: Visual7/E+/Getty Images; 168: CO Leong/Shutterstock; 169 CR: Yuriy Kulik/Shutterstock; 170: Adam Forster/EyeEm/Getty Images; 171 Bkgrd: Brian Hoffman/Alamy

Stock Photo; 171 BR: Amble Design/Shutterstock; 171 TR: Hero Images/Getty Images; 172 BR: Kwiktor/iStock/Getty Images; 172 TR: Douglas Klug/Moment/Getty Images; 173 BR: Brais Seara/Moment Open/Getty Images; 173 TR: Peter Mulligan/Moment/Getty Images; 174 BC: Jim Cumming/Moment/Getty Images; 174 BR: Colleen Gara/Moment/Getty Images; 174 TC: Amble Design/Shutterstock; 176 Bkgrd: Marco Pozzi Photographer/Moment/Getty Images; 176 BR: Amble Design/Shutterstock; 177 Bkgrd: CliqueImages/DigitalVision/Getty Images; 177 TR: Hero Images/Getty Images; 178: Visual7/E+/Getty Images; 180 BR: Iain Masterton/Alamy Stock Photo; 180 CR: Tony McLean/Moment/Getty Images; 182: Herraez/iStock/Getty Images

Topic 6

184: Karel Gallas/Shutterstock; 185 BC: Miraswonderland/Fotolia; 185 BL: Andrii Rafalskyi/123RF; 185 BR: Dixi/Fotolia; 186 BC: Ben Queenborough/Shutterstock; 186 BL: Renamarie/123RF; 186 BR: Henk Bentlage/Shutterstock; 186 TR: Michaeljung/Shutterstock; 188 CR: SzaszFabian Jozsef/Fotolia; 188 TCR: Denboma/Fotolia; 189: Chiyacat/Shutterstock; 190: Tofino/Alamy Stock Photo; 191 BR: Zoonar GmbH/Alamy Stock Photo; 191 C: Johannes Hansen/Alamy Stock Photo; 191 CL: Fotohunter/Shutterstock; 192 BL: Amophoto_au/Shutterstock; 192 BR: Denis and Yulia Pogostins/Shutterstock; 192 C: Nattika/Shutterstock; 193 BC: Michaeljung/Shutterstock; 193 C: Vladimir Wrangel/Shutterstock; 193 CR: Ger Bosma/Moment Open/Getty Images; 193 TC: Trabantos/Shutterstock; 194 B: Igor Janicek/Shutterstock; 194 C: Michaeljung/Shutterstock; 197 CL: Elenathewise/Fotolia; 197 CR: Teemu Tretjakov/Fotolia; 198 B: Eric Gevaert/Fotolia; 198 Bkgrd: Krivosheev Vitaly/Shutterstock; 199 BL: PhilipYb Studio/Shutterstock; 199 BR: Viktor Kunz/123RF; 200 B: Nataliya Nazarova/Shutterstock; 200 TR: Anrymos/Fotolia; 201 B: Mikaelmales/Fotolia; 201 CR: Michaeljung/Shutterstock; 202: Julija Sapic/Fotolia; 203 BC: EmiliaUngur/Shutterstock; 203 BCL: WilleeCole Photography/Shutterstock; 203 BCR: Wiktord/Shutterstock; 203 BR: Grigorita Ko/Shutterstock; 203 BR: Tobkatrina/123RF; 203 CL: Jarobike/Shutterstock; 203 CR: Grigorita Ko/Fotolia; 203 TL: Michaeljung/Shutterstock; 204: Milica Nistoran/Shutterstock; 205: Ralko/Shutterstock; 206: Old Apple/Shutterstock; 208 B: Sergey Krasnoshchokov/Shutterstock; 208 C: Debbie Steinhausser/Shutterstock; 208 TR: Rudmer Zwerver/Shutterstock; 209 BC: Michaeljung/Shutterstock; 209 CR: FloridaStock/Shutterstock; 209 TL: Gerrit_de_Vries/Shutterstock; 210 B: Paul Farnfield/123RF; 210 T: Kelsey Green/Shutterstock; 211 BL: Aussieanouk/Fotolia; 211 BR: Koldunova/Fotolia; 211 T: Idiz/Shutterstock; 212 L: Johannes Lodewikus Van Der Merwe/123RF; 212 R: Mark Bridger/Shutterstock; 213 B: 123RF; 213 CR: Orhan Cam/123RF; 213 TR: Andras Deak/123RF; 214 B: Debbie Steinhausser/Shutterstock; 214 CR: Richard Seeley/Shutterstock; 214 TL: Michaeljung/Shutterstock; 215 CL: Uwimages/Fotolia; 215 CR: Trubavink/Fotolia; 216 Bkgrd: Polarpx/Shutterstockj; 216 BR: Michaeljung/Shutterstock; 216 TC: Ben Queenborough/Shutterstock; 216 TL: Renamarie/123RF; 216 TR: Henk Bentlage/Shutterstock; 217 B: Sara Winter/Fotolia; 217 TR: WavebreakMediaMicro/Fotolia; 218 BL: Stocker1970/Shutterstock; 218 BR: AJF Natural Collection/Alamy Stock Photo; 218 C: 816115/Shutterstock; 218 T: Jonathan Pledger/Shutterstock; 221: Ljusi/iStock/Getty Images; 222: Scenic Shutterbug/Shutterstock

Credits

End Matter

EM0 BR: Cagla Acikgoz/Shutterstock; EM0 CR: Tyler Boyes/Shutterstock; EM0 TR: Sergey Kuznetsov/123RF; EM1: Ted Kinsman/Science Source; EM2 BC: Evgeny Mishustin/Alamy Stock Photo; EM2 BL: Gjermund/Shutterstock; EM2 BR: Zcw/Shutterstock; EM2 CR: Karuka/Shutterstock; EM3 BR: Vvoe/Shutterstock; EM3 TR: Robbie Shone/Aurora/Getty Images; EM4: Adam Burton/robertharding/Getty Images; EM5: Ermess/Shutterstock; EM6: Snapgalleria/Shutterstock; EM7: Simone Brandt/Alamy Stock Photo; EM8 C: 123RF; EM8 TR: Shawn Hempel/Alamy Stock Photo; EM9: Lloyd Sutton/Alamy Stock Photo; EM10: Alessandro Colle/Shutterstock; EM11 BR: DonNichols/E+/Getty Images; EM11 C: Flegere/Shutterstock; EM11 TR: Zelenskaya/Shutterstock; EM12: Fat Jackey/Shutterstock; EM13: Martin Barraud/Caiaimage/GettyImages; EM14: Mark Bridger/Shutterstock; EM15: Hero Images/Getty Images; EM16: Brian A Jackson/iStock/Getty Images; EM17: S7chvetik/Shutterstock; EM18: Pavle Marjanovic/Shutterstock; EM19: Debbie Steinhausser/Shutterstock; EM20: Isabelle Bonaire/Fotolia; EM21: AlinaMD/Shutterstock; EM22: Carloscastilla/iStock/Getty Images

My Notes and Designs

Draw, Write, Create